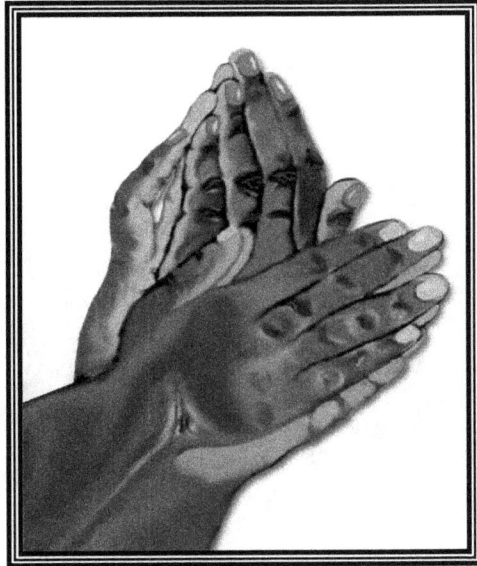

May The Lord move in your spirit as you read
Facts Of Life According To The Word Volume 1

Facts Of Life According To The Word

Volume 1

By

Carol Beck

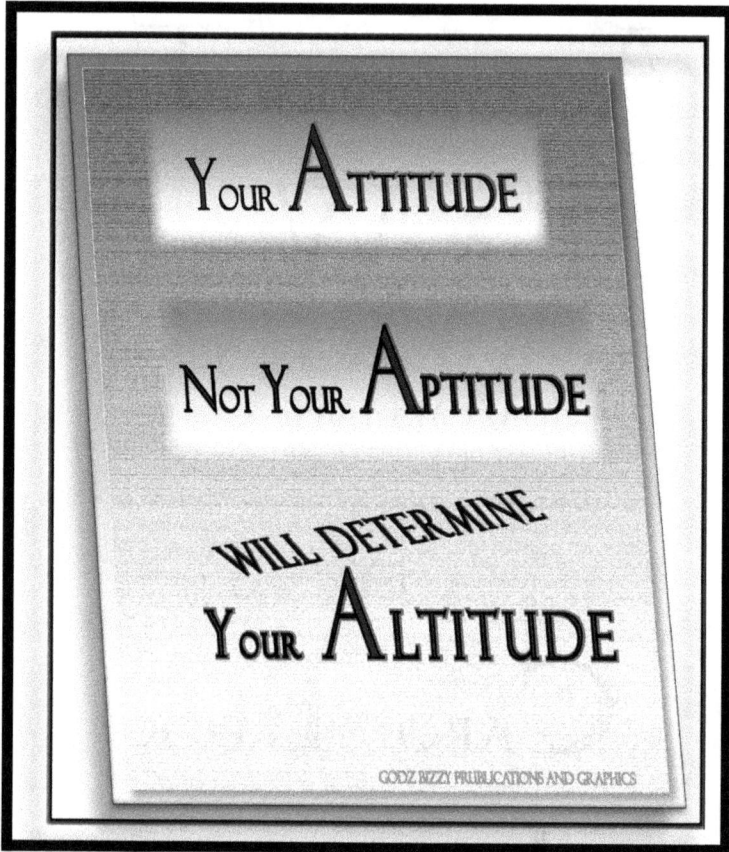

COPYRIGHT

GODZ BIZZY
PUBLICATIONS

ISBN 0-9717173-0-3

90000

9 780971 717305

DEDICATION

Facts Of Life According To The Word is dedicated to my late Grandmother, Mabel Matthews. The impact of her constantly correcting my use of the English language and my behavior as a person, paid off. Also, her praying for my salvation has been answered.

I only wish she were here so that I could give her a super sized hug, and a great big thank you from the bottom of my heart.

About The Author

lthough, I was aware of the amazing intervention coming into my life inspiring the writing of Facts Of Life According to the Word, I still questioned it. The feeling that was upon me appeared strange seeing that I felt I was not, in any way, qualified to be used by God. I had not lived a saintly lifestyle, and was not acknowledging the Golden Rule. As a matter of fact, I had moved far beyond...going in the opposite direction.

I was a practicing Buddhist. For 5 years, I diligently devoted my life to one and a half hours every morning, and forty five minutes every evening kneeling before a small wooden shine that contained a scroll of a dead language. On the front outside of the open door box, was a tray of incense ashes that was filling to the rim from the many days of chanting Nam Myo Ho Renge Kyo. The most precious of fruits was freshly placed in a bowl beside the incense daily. A string of beads was positioned neatly at the front of the meticulous set up. Lying next to the beads, to be held during the praying procession, was a the small booklet that contained the words to be chanted.

This had become my routine after being introduced by a new acquaintance attempting to reach out offering me help in my time of anguish. I had fallen into a state of despair because of the loss of my business, cars, and home. All my worldly goods were gone. My thoughts were, "What else can possibly happen."

Being a person who has displayed the strength to lead throughout my entire life, I never figured myself to be one that could be taken to such an extreme as practicing Buddhism. I know my cut off points, and will generally not let anyone take me beyond them. However, my strength is that of a human. My power does not exceed the power of Him who created me. With that said, I found myself in a yielding position.

At what I felt was the height of my disillusionment, a sudden feeling, came over me. It was solid. An unwavering transformation was taking place. A voice was speaking to me, but the voice was silent. I could only hear it on the inside of me. There was a soft shoving with no feeling of physical contact. It was a motivation that moved me to another level of life. It was God working through me. It was most astonishing.

Being raised in the Hebrew faith gave me some enlightenment. However, as is with many young people being forced to attend church, the information went into one ear, and out of the other....'so I thought'. It was not until the period during the writing of Facts Of Life According To The Word that I realized quite a bit of what I had learned was trapped inside. I've termed this section of my mind, that retains pertinent information, a mental file cabinet. It could have been Gods' way of preparing me for this journey in my life. The file cabinet has opened and the Good News is pouring out.

Solomon said something that quite possibly could apply to

me.

Proverbs 22: 6

Train a child in the way he should go, and when he is old he will not turn from it.

In chronological years, I would be considered old, but in Gods' eyes I'm obviously being considered worthy to be a vessel pouring out facts juxtaposing the Word of God in today's lifestyle. It is intended for anyone having ears to hear.

That is my mission. That is who I am today.

ACKNOWLEDGEMENT

To the greatest power in the world, my Father in Heaven--the Creator of All, I give tremendous thanks. "This could not have been done without the guidance of your Holy Spirit towards true enlightenment."

To my three younger daughters who were still living at home and delighted in having chapters read to them as they were completed; showing great enthusiasm and patience while Our Father used me to do my share in spreading the Good News. May the Lord Bless them, keeping them healthy, safe, and prosperous as they grow in His Word; relying, trusting and keeping Him in the number one position of their lives. To my eldest daughter who has gasped the Lord, realizing and utilizing His Power in every move that she makes; May she continue to experience His unending Grace.

To the lady from Albertson's, "Annette, you are my first recognized experience with a prophetess. Your obedience to the Will of God has put you in unshakable standing. Your seed has been planted into fertile soil. May the Lord Bless you with all that He promises to those that submit to His Will, and Commands."

To my dear Gangster acquaintance: Sharing the plight of the Motel 6 in Atlanta GA, "Tony, you didn't know you were being used by God. Don't be shocked, I didn't know either. I wasn't moving on the book fast enough, so the Lord used you to urge me along. Thank you! May the Lord Bless you, Angela and the kids according to your goodness which is far more than you realize."

To all the wonderful people that helped to keep me focused, showing sincere concern in the production of the Facts of Life According to the Word, "May Jehovah God show forth His Grace, and in His own time, lift you up to Heaven on the Wings of His mightiest Angels."

Amen

TABLE OF CONTENTS

Facts of Life According To The Word Volume 1
By Carol Beck

PROLOGUE

Facts Of Life According To The Word Volume I applies an autobiographical approach to an investigation of the link between the modern individual and certain Christian principles. It juxtaposes scriptural interpretation with a personal narrative centering on incidents from the authors' life in an effort to portray a viable role for faith in an often confusing contemporary social and political landscape.

It opens by describing an incident in Las Vegas when the author and her husband were in a rather desperate state as a result of his being out of work. An encounter with a woman named Jeannette lead her away from Buddhism toward Christianity, a change that also contributed to her decision to record her thoughts.

Next in a discussion of youth and gangs, she

points to the family unit as a possible solution, asserting that a child should have 'the loving relationship of two parents at once.' Chapter six touches upon the disadvantages that doubt in the Word of God presents.

In Facts Of Life According To The Word Volume II, the author focuses on 'Love', indicating particular biblical passages meant to illustrate a belief that such an ideal constitutes the first and most important of all the Commandments...and ...virtually the only way of finding peace in this world. An exploration of a more negative emotion renders a look at 'The Death of Jesus Christ' as an example of how He showed us the love that Jehovah has for His creation, by submitting himself to the anger that Satan had place in the hearts of mankind.'

Promoting the adoption of a higher power as part of an overall path grounded on a sense of healing and renewal, Facts Of Life According To The Word Volumes I & II contemplates the human capacity for change. The text spans an array of topics, from parenting

and family concerns to capitalism and 'worldliness.'

        As a whole, Facts Of Life According To The Word Volumes I & II, using the authors experiences is designed to enlighten and inspire the reader who may be considering similar questions.

This Prologue has been written by
an editor of an undisclosed publishing company

DESTINY OR FATE

Waking up in the luxurious Sahara Hotel on the Las Vegas Strip would probably have been a happening thing for some people, but not for us. It had become our unplanned temporary home.

Glaring at the clock to make sure we hadn't overslept, I stumbled over to the patio window. As I looked out at the pool attendants preparing to service the many guests displaying an appearance of being financially able to be there, I could hear my husbands voice in the background urging me, "Get dressed, we have to pick up a money gram."

I looked over at my Budhsadon; the wooden shrine which contained a scroll of a dead language attached to the inside back wall that's used as a focal point. Feeling I needed to chant because right now we needed some serious benefits from the Universe, I waved my hand in an, "It's okay motion." We were already cutting it close. We had a deadline to keep, and time didn't permit my normal morning devotion.

It was prophesied to me that I would write this book. At the time of this occurrence I thought, "This must be the most bazaar thing that I have heard yet." It was not because I doubted that I could write a book, but the person telling me that God was calling me to do this did not have the resemblance of someone I would hear anything from. I was overly confident in myself. Anyone wishing to enhance my level of intelligence would have to be endowed with an appearance of intellectual superiority. Obviously I had to learn that God doesn't look at people from the outside, He searches ones heart for goodness.

Here we are in a customer service line in an

Albertson's grocery store. My husband, Dennis and I, were pretty much stuck in Las Vegas needing serious help. Being in the store on this day to pick up a money gram sent to us by one of the numerous people that helped us during this desperate time; trying not to think about our predicament brought on by the loss of my husband's job, and in a rejoicing mood, because we were being bailed out for the next two days, my spirits were up.

In line behind us was a lady waiting to cash her check. Her nails were extremely long, and polished gold with tiny gold ornamented decals. As I complemented her on their uniqueness, I was opening a door that I would have never imagined. She and I began to talk about her nails which lead to her telling me, and now Dennis who had started listening, but not really paying close attention, about her recent graduation from cosmetology school. It turned out that she, whose name was Jeanette Robinson, had accepted Jesus into her life, and He was making a great impact on her once meager existence. Her excitement was unusually refreshing as she began to testify about the wonderful ways that God was working in her daily affairs.

Under normal circumstances, I would not have

been interested in hearing Jeanette's confessions, or testimonies, as I later learned they are referred too. I was not a practicing Christian (a person that believes in Jesus Christ), nor did I attend a church that worshipped Jesus. On the other hand, I've always felt Dennis was that sort of guy when it suited him. He was raised Catholic; attending Catholic Schools, but if what he wanted to do did not conform with the Golden Rule, it got kicked to the curb until he was ready to use the Word of God to his advantage again. Dennis had begun listening with both ears and I thought, "Oh no! Now I'm stuck until he's had enough."

We finished our business, and naturally feeling more relaxed knowing that we had the funds to secure our living expense for the next two days, we waited for Jeanette to finish her transaction.

Jeanette continued raving to us about the wonderful things God had done for her. How she had sunk into the muddy mire's of life, and had been excommunicated from society. Her BMW driving husband still tending bar in one the major resort hotels on the Las Vegas Strip, refusing to accept Jesus, was still on the scene. She had been involved in a sorted variety of self degrading activities which lead to her losing her mind. She admitted that she had become totally incoherent. The picture she painted was gruesome but interesting. I felt pity for her past. It sounded hopeless, but then she was rescued by Jesus, and saved from the pit of Hell.

"Whenever I've had a problem with a hairstyle in school," she said, "I'd take my Bible and go into the bathroom to read the Word. I'd ask Jesus to help me to do these Finger Waves so that I could pass this test, and I'd come back out and top everybody's style.

"My credit was ruined, and the Lord gave me that brand new car over there; the white one! See? Next to the blue one!"
She continued as she pointed out across the parking lot of Albertson's. If I had really know Jesus I would have said , "Praise the Lord," but instead, in my carnal mind I said, "Wow, that's great!"

As Dennis and I stood there listening to Jeanette, my mind started drifting back to our situation. I began thinking, "What are we going to do after this little money runs out." My body was becoming anxious, and I was ready to leave. I looked over at Dennis to give him the, "Let's go cue", only to see that he was totally engrossed with this one sided conversation.

"Oh boy, he's finally found someone who is taking his side against me," I thought. "It's time to put a stop to this."

The fact that I wasn't a Christian and he was, caused me to have these feelings, plus the fact that I felt that he has used God in the past to try to manipulate me.

The early morning partial sun was turning into an afternoon heat wave. August in Las Vegas was neither the place nor the season to be standing outside on a parking lot talking. We had obviously been there conversing for a couple of hours. Dennis and I started out early that morning so that we could pick the money up, and take care of our hotel expense. I had not anticipated getting involved in such a lengthy conversation with this stranger.

"Dennis, don't we have something to do?' I asked.

He mildly brushed me off, which is what he normally does when he doesn't want to hear what I have to say. Jeanette stepped in before I had a chance to respond, and it's a good thing she did.

"The Lord has something for you to do," she said

smiling.

"I don't think so, "I replied, "You see, I am a Latter Day Buddhist. I chant Nam Myo Ho Renge Kyo to the Power of the Universe. I do not pray to Jesus, nor do I acknowledge Him."

She replied, "I don't down anybody's beliefs, but I'll tell you this, the Lord is calling you, and you will respond because He has a job for you to do."

"Okay!" I said sarcastically, "And what is that?"

"You are going to write a book."

"Is that right!"

Forcing myself to maintain a cool and collected composure, as well as to pretend to play along with this show, I asked, "What's it going to be about?"

By this time, I was looking at her out of the side of my face as I customarily do when a person has gone a little too far; presuming to know me better than I know myself. I was already ticked off with Dennis for not acknowledging my request to leave earlier. I felt he wanted somebody--anybody to help him bring me back to the Lord. This was right on time for him. I felt his motives were dishonorable. His desire was to point out how a wife should be totally submissive regardless of what the husband does, or don't do.

At this point, Jeanette announced, "Let's pray!" This was the final straw.
"I don't pray, like you pray," I said. "I told you, I practice Buddhism."

How could I allow myself to be sucked into this. It was times like this when I wished that I could be really mean and heartless; at least put my foot down to people intruding my personal mind space. I could be pretty vicious to Dennis because he knew better. He knew what I believed in, and I felt he was taking advantage of the moment. I couldn't be mean to Jeanette. She didn't really give me a reason to be. I've always delighted in someone's good fortune. She was verbally sharing the story of her good fortune with us. No personal crime in that.

Dennis extended his hand outward to connect with her hand which was already in position to receive it. He then reached over and grabbed my hand in his normal demanding manner. My mind was racing with thoughts,

"The nerve of him. Let me just do this and get it over

with. When we get back to the car, I'm going to chew him up, and spit him out verbally. He's always trying to control me. Look at all of these people passing us by; walking around us--looking at us like we're crazy. Here we are standing in the middle of the entrance way of a large Albertson's grocery store at high noon in a three--person group prayer. What can these people be thinking?" The embarrassment was too much for me. "Let this hurry and be over with. Maybe If I close my eyes, I won't be able to see the people looking at us, and the expressions on their faces. They're probably thinking we came to Las Vegas and gambled our money away. Hummh, we didn't have any when we got here. This woman will finish this praying exhibition, let my hand go, and I can run to the car and hide. I'm sure glad I don't live in this area."
"Everyone in agreement, say Amen", she concluded "Yeah! It's over!"

With the same positive, without a doubt attitude that she possessed throughout the entire conversation, she looked at me intently, reminding me that regardless of what I thought, or to whom I was praying, the Lord wanted me back, and He would get me back soon. Guess what? God did intervene in a very noticeable way.

One month later, while still in Las Vegas, I found myself in a state of confusion over this matter. Although one would say that someone committed to a religion such as Buddhism for five years, which requires devotion and extreme dedication would pretty much be deep seated in their beliefs; a desire came upon me to read the Bible. Fortunately, Dennis had brought along with him a copy of the Original African Heritage Edition of the Holy Bible. Jeanette had suggested that God was calling me. However, I know from past experiences that I'm not a follower, nor do I do anything that I don't want to do. God in His mysteriousness worked in my life, and I have written this book which He inspired. He has been present throughout opening my mind to His Will.

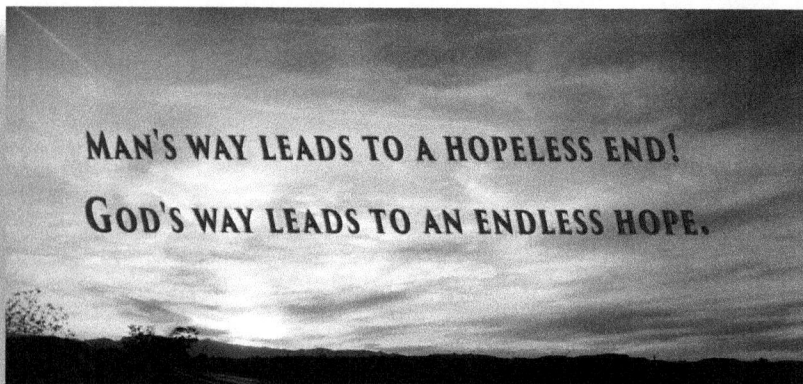

MAN'S WAY LEADS TO A HOPELESS END!
GOD'S WAY LEADS TO AN ENDLESS HOPE.

L_{IFE} A_S I S_{EE} I_T

L ife! How I love it. Unpredictable! Indeed it is! Bringing many levels of emotions constantly. Everyday is a new experience. However, a wrong decision can affect life so dramatically, but a right choice can bring heavenly rewards.

Once I seriously began writing one year later, I realized that my trials and tribulations contributed greatly to my calling. Compiling the necessary information for this book reflects years of personal lessons acquired through worldly experience; research, involvement of various spiritual beliefs, points of interest taken from motivational speeches, and hours of church sermons.

Personally, I believe myself to be a hands--on--person. I have truly been involved in many things, good and bad. Let's see how you sum up your own life's endeavors when you've finished reading Facts Of Life According To The Word.

PURPOSE AND GOALS IN ONES LIFE

I've learned enough not to claim to know all the answers. My curiosity and spirituality encourages me to continue to seek more defined ways to learn and fulfill ones purpose in life. One very simple way as a beginning point would be: Evaluate what you have done in your life, decide which of these things you've enjoyed doing best naturally, or without formal training. For skills or talents that you may have been trained to perform, determine how easy they were to learn. Now you've got a general picture.

It's my belief that everyone has been given an innate talent that reflects pure goodness. This would be the area that one would expound on in life's endeavors. We'll elaborate more on, bringing out in detail, your precise God given purpose in this life later in coming chapters. One should always seek adequate information to make an intelligent decision, especially seeing that this is the first day of the rest of your life. Let's start taking it seriously. It's been revealed to me, there will be a judgment call. We'll all have to answer for our decisions.

Everyone has a destiny in life that has been preset for them. However, we set goals for our lives as well. Those of us that are motivated set out to accomplish them. Gaining intellectual information from institutions of higher learning offers great gain in some cases, but there is a flip side to the coin.

Many people acquire higher education only to realize they have chosen a field that they're no longer interested in; sometimes before completion. There are times that we don't quite reach our goal before we have a switch turned on in our heads, and-- or our hearts. It will usually be due to some recent dramatic change that have taken place in our lives. This could come about because of a wrong decision brought on by insufficient knowledge, or it could be ignited by the up's and down's of the stock markets producing a economic inflationary result. Maybe it's caused by the changes this world is rapidly experiencing. Actually the world progressed from the horse and carriage stage, to the space age level, and then into a high technology zone in a little over a half century. The rapid speed is definitely something to consider when planning and pursuing your goals. The employment field that was available yesterday is no longer in existence.

I've been experiencing a tremendous turn of events taking place since this calling in my life. This has caused me to become more aware of the changing world around me. It certainly is not to say that I have not seen changes previously, but I'm realizing the present negative influence is, by far, more acceptable as a way of life. Things are spiraling out of control. I'm wondering who is running God's Creation here. This world has become so corrupt and evil. It's difficult to know when to extend kindness to anyone. Everyone is playing a game to win. The one that comes out on top is the winner. He'll be holding more cards than the looser. It doesn't matter who they're hurting to achieve their goal. The point is, it's a rat race out here. We have become so acclimated to the dysfunctions that it seems normal.

Political parties are in battles with one another in this great United States of America. Instead of serving the people, they are serving themselves. There's a power struggle going on right before our eyes. We have governing parties competing unfairly against each other. It has become such a normal everyday occurrence that many citizens pay very little attention to it anymore. Such travesties are printed and aired on TV news shows, but nothing much is done to prevent it from being repeated by the next elected or appointed official that will enter into the commanding office of this wonderfully free country.

I haven't researched this particular subject, but how many times have we heard of the President of our great nation having an affair outside of his marriage with not one woman, but two, and possibly more. The news media pounced on this as though it has never been done before. In our past, we've had a president whom we loved, that was involved in adulterous relationships. Somehow it didn't seem to be as newsworthy until many years later. In 1998 we were repeating the same episode. The major difference is the president of the United States faced impeachment. Fast forward to 2014. We have an African American serving a 2nd term as President of the United States of America whose success is being blocked because of the color of his skin.

Returning to what I spoke of previously. Everyone is playing a game to win. If the opposing party could have achieved what they really wanted, there would have been no need to expose possible sexual indiscreetness on our president's part. If they could have kept control of government in Washington D.C., they would have no need to keep the citizens of the United States facing a constant condition of fiscal economic collapse. Their hatred of the skin color of our leader has caused very bizarre behavior. What are they trying to achieve? The winning hand. It doesn't matter that they are discrediting our country's top commander, and placing us under a microscope to be humiliated and frown on by the entire world. This is our country. It is indeed, blessed by God, being formed and based on Biblical principles by men that respected and honored God. However, we seem to be determined to lower our standards to comply with behaviors that are from the dark side.

Grown educated leaders of our country, that we, with our democracy process, have put into positions to lead us, are either committing suicide, or being killed to keep from answering questions about their involvement in underhanded endeavors. As one of my friends so eloquently said in poetry, the white robes of the Ku Klux Klan has been traded in for the black robes of justice. The ordinary little guy doesn't know who to vote for these days. Everybody's acting. Large corporations sink money into organizations such as the American Legislative Exchange Council to promote laws that will ensure the success of their business. It's simple; They vote for the candidate that's for sale. That candidate will go along with whatever that company needs to happen to be successful.

I've given considerable thought to our voting process. I've reached a point that I really didn't care who got into office because whatever they said always had a way of changing by the time they take the judicial seat; for whatever reason. This by no means is the democratic way. Knowing how important each individual vote is, I should not allow my disillusionments to hinder exercising the right afforded me as a citizen. But will it really count? To use our right to vote is suppose to be the only way we can keep our country from falling into a dictatorship rule. Here in 2014, it feels like we're tittering on the edge of a dictatorship government.

Things such as these have caused my life's goals to change. I have a desire to do something that will help people that suffer with a feeling of hopelessness to know there is a way of bringing an assured and positive outlook back into their lives. If they've never had it, Facts of Life According To The Word Volume I & II will be quite refreshing to them. If they have, and have strayed onto another path, hopefully their memory will be jarred, as have mine.

It is predestined for me to be on the course that I'm currently on. To describe this metaphorically, I'm walking in shoes that fit perfectly. There is no pinch. My walk is pure, good, and will produce a helping hand to lost souls, as well as, self satisfaction to me. This could only have been obtained with a renewing of my thought pattern. The mind has got to be correct; being inspired by the Holy Spirit.

PARENTING TODAY

Being a parent, I must say my concerns extends greatly towards the children. Their minds are becoming corrupted at young ages. The media with their blatantly uncensored influence has been extremely damaging. In the name of free speech they glorify evil. They offer television entertainment wrapped in shiny packages that have blood, violence, and sex dripping from every scene. It sends an, "It's okay" message to our children to be violent and promiscuous beginning in their preteens. As a matter of fact, it looks pretty cool to a child. He doesn't know any better. For the most part, the TV is the baby-sitter.

For many reasons, parents are not able to stay at

home with their children. The most obvious is the cost of living which has increased to the point that every two parent family household needs a job of at least two incomes just to live in the ghetto. If they want to live in a decent neighborhood, they each need two jobs, or at least an additional income per parent. One hardly has time for their child if they're working one job. Two jobs offer better housing, but even less parental guidance.

The schools can't be relied on to do the work of the parents. They can barely be relied on to do what they're suppose to do because of non parental involvement, plus the disillusionment of what the educators original intentions were. We know from the amount of money that our teachers are paid, they did not decide on teaching as a career to become millionaires. They must have had a vision of educating our youth. If you're a concerned parent, you know that you've got to have a good conversational link going on between yourself, and your child so you can stay on top of what's going on in school, as well as, who their friends are. You already have two jobs, well here's your third job.

This has become quite tiring now. You're working these ridiculous amount of hours. What little money you're making taxation is taking. You're stressed out wearing all of the different hats that's required of you at the same time. You are concerned about your status on the job. Maybe you are dedicated to your employers, but you just can't give anything more towards proving it. Now the company decides they're paying too much financial income out. They circulate an interoffice memo with this announcement:

MEMO

TO: All Employees With Less Than

Five Years On The Job

SUBJECT: The Yearly Report

Our Company's Current 'Yearly Report' Shows Expenditures Exceeding Profits. We are sorry to inform you, there will be a down sizing of the company's employees starting at your level to go into effect immediately. Your next paycheck will be your final. Your services will no longer be necessary at this time. Thank you for your understanding.

You have just been laid off. In the next two months, the company brings in kids, just out of college, giving them your jobs at entry level pay. Not a thing you can do about it, even if you did know. This would have to be proven to make a case. Meanwhile, you are so preoccupied with this situation that you've lost touch with your children. They have picked up a couple of friends of bad character that you were not aware of.

Your phone rings, it's the police. They are holding your child at the police station along with another kid. They were picked up for shoplifting. Your kid was guilty of being there with the shoplifter. Although, he didn't actually steal anything, he'll still have to go before the judge. He's considered an 'Accessory to the Fact.'

Now is when you find out about this new law that your state has passed requiring parents to assume any financial responsibility for their child's actions. You already know about the law that forbids you to chastise your child, and so does he. I am a parent of five children and totally against child abuse, but this law has challenged us to determine what constitutes child abuse. It was important to me that my children grew up with values, and respect for themselves as well as others. I didn't spare the rod because I wasn't going to spoil the child. Before anyone goes left, thinking that I beat children with a rod, hear what's written in the Bible about disciplining a child.

> Proverbs 13:24
> He who spares the rod hates his son, but he who loves
> him is careful to discipline him.

In this life a spoiled child is doomed unless the parents have an adequate amount of money to sustain the whims of a kid, as well as, to pay for the problems of the attitude that is produced from excessive permissiveness.

The tolerance level of people today, as a whole, is escalating rapidly. We complain about the situation but we continue accepting it. By and large we've given up hope. the children punish the parents when they don't go along with the program. Some parents are intimidated by their children, therefore, they fear them. The parents at that point release their power to the child, and the child then adds that to their already corrupt personality, and release it on some other undeserving soul. This is partially the reason for gun related violence. Not just a simple little hand gun, but automatic weapons with capabilities to discharge large amounts of ammunition in very short periods of time. Bullets that are designed to explode tearing up the flesh once they enter the human body. Sounds gruesome doesn't it? You may not know about the viciousness of the varieties of weapons and ammunition being produced that actually make their way to the streets to be sold to our children. Don't be shocked that your child may know.

Gun manufacturers are upgrading power weapons almost as fast as computers are being upgraded. Every six months a computer is outdated unless a chip is added. It seems to me, a newer and more powerful gun is being released to go onto the market at least once a year. In certain neighborhoods. It appears as though the younger the child is, the quicker the information of the latest style of gun, and where to purchase it, is rapidly available to them. One would think they were on display in the window of a department store in the mall. (I had to laugh at that). I don't think they have gun shops in the malls. Really, it isn't funny though. It's real!

We have seen drugs escalate to an all time high at a rapid rate recently. The drugs don't choose a particular class or economic level to infiltrate. One can be assured, at the top of the ladder of the distribution of these mind altering substances sit some of our most powerful and influential families. They are capitalizing off the destruction of their fellow human beings. Whatever happened to the Biblical principles that made this country so great. Parents beware! There is a force lurking outside. It wishes to devour our children. The attack is great, but we have the ability to stop this evil.

PEOPLE DON'T GIVE UP

The noticeable increase in homeless people that line the streets of our metropolitan cities has increased tremendously. It is astonishing to learn the amount of these people that have been forced into sleeping and eating arrangements that are beneath humane conditions. Many of them suffer with mental or physical illnesses'. Some become addicted to mind altering substances that caused a spiraling into darkness. Some were forced out of their homes because of the downfall of the economy. The Street People sometimes move, from location to location, carrying their belongings in shopping carts. They feed themselves on scraps from public garbage cans while tons of meticulously prepared meals, handled only by trained chefs, are being tossed in the trash.

I've seen and wondered why hotels, country clubs, exclusive resorts, and convention centers deprive the homeless of these untouched, unused prepared meals that they no longer have use of. I was informed that they're afraid of being sued if an illness occurs.

The government has cut help programs for the needy, and have made it more difficult for the agendas still in existence to provide assistance to deserving people needing help.

What causes people to give into vices that are destructive? The illusion of excitement and glamour along with the lack of foresight of what's to come. Why are people who are on the right path allowing or tolerating this decline in our society? It's predestined for the world to be on this course. It is absolutely amazing, the amount of people that are not clued in to the Creation; God's purpose for His World, what has been, and what is to come. If we fully knew, the world would be excitingly different. We would have a life of assurance, love, happiness, and contentment as we stand firm. There would be no wars or racial problems; neither drug abuse, hunger nor homelessness, and no worry over what will be today or tomorrow. Everyone would have a positive outlook on life because life would be blissfully wonderful. It is very difficult to envision this because of what the majority of us have been conditioned to deal with on a daily basis from birth. In simpler words; how we've been trained to think.

As it is, people form opinions, likes, and dislikes about other people based on race, religion, economic positions, a neighborhood a person may live in, or have come from. It can become so trivial that people judge others because of the clothes they wear, or the size of their nose, eyes or lips. This is sad, truly sad. Not one person on earth is free of problems. They are brought on by the way we think; the way we react to events that occur in our lives. From the richest and most powerful, to the poorest and most impoverished, we all share unfortunate occurrences in our lives. These bleak times can last indefinitely or for short periods. They can be viewed as major or minor in magnitude depending on our minds. Yes! The mind plays a major role in how we first perceive, and then exist. Change your way of thinking and change your life.

As I see it, we have no choice. If we want this world to improve, and our lives to improve. We must change our way of thinking and readjust our priorities.

That's How I See Life. In my mind, that's how it is!

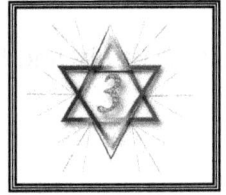

GANGSTER LIFE

D riving through the mountains of Northern Arizona; my eyes resting upon the beauty of Gods' Creation, I began thinking about the problems of the world. What gave entry to these thoughts were the beautiful virgin landscapes that I had now become a part of through this magnificent tour. It was like being in another world. I began to wonder if human feet had ever touched this extraordinary terrain. The mountains and rolling hills appeared so magnificently undisturbed. My mind became extremely overwhelmed as I thought about the fact that God created all of this, and then He created us so that we could enjoy it, live in it, rule it, multiply and flourish. How He must love us.

Continuing to enjoy the splendor of the mountains blending with the beautiful clear blue skies, and defined patches of clouds appearing as puffy cotton sheets separated into pockets throughout, my mind wandered to God's purpose for my life. The magic of the moment directed my mind towards young people in our society who are growing up with false values and impulsive views on life. Many only being exposed to urban life; not traveling outside of their neighborhoods, much less the city limits. Others not caring what's outside of the Hood. My heart goes out to them. I have a desire to help these young people develop self worth; To make them aware that they have an alternative to the limitations in which they find themselves.

Lack of positive leadership has caused chaos in many of our neighborhoods across the nation. The realization and wonders of God have somehow evaded people who are to set examples. They are not doing their jobs. Quite possibly, the approach to get this information across to our future leaders is all wrong. After all, communication breakdowns are common from generation to generation.

As we continued to drive, the feeling of peacefulness became intense. An overwhelming passion enveloped me wanting everyone to feel this, or at least know that it exist. Everything in life is not a hustle bustle, or dog eat dog. You don't have to live life with a negative attitude. How wonderful calmness and peace can be. How wonderful it would be if we all came together with this in mind. As the savoring feeling of freedom from mental and emotional distress saturated my body, words of profound meaning began to flow into my mind:

GANGSTER RAP:

Let your mind be enlightened
Leave the destruction of the lost and unsaved,
and come into the light.

Let yourself be changed by breaking off that old you
and putting on the protection of God.

He is the power with the master plan
He offers unconditional love.
When you accept Him, He makes you His child.

He is down with the righteous divine dope.,
Give you a high of glory, joy, and saving that last forever.

Fulfill your purpose,
Honor your Creator,
Receive His Love freely without risking your life.

Give it up to the eternal power,
Young brothers and sisters.
Live in the presence of the Father
Under His Mighty Right Hand and
Delight in having all your dreams and desires fulfilled.

WHAT'S UP WITH GANGSTER LIFE

Our young people join gangs for various reasons: Parents spending more time on their jobs away from their children; leaving the children with idle time to submit to the evil and negativity of peer pressure. Parents who are on drugs and preoccupied with their own obsessions. One parent families who are not capable of fulfilling the many tasks of the dual parent household.

God did not intend for one parent to raise a child. Both the parent and the child are cheated out of the beauty of a family. One parent is pressured with all the responsibilities and doesn't get a chance to enjoy the nurturing of the child, and the child is deprived of having the loving relationship of two parents at once.

Children that lack positive means of excitement in life, and decide to embark upon methods of negative excitement as the way to go.
- A need to belong to a group, so they join a gang...
- Consistently low life-styles, not realizing that all situations can be overcome...
- Boredom... Tired of feeling hopelessly in a no win position...
- Depressed - not accepting the light ..
- Improper guidance...

- Low self Esteem...
- Being raised with hopeless attitudes...
- And the list goes on.

And we ask why the world is in such turmoil? Why are we so slighted if Our Father wants to do all of these wonderful things, and is so capable.

IT'S YOUR CALL

From the beginning of time, our marvelous and glorious Father has given us the privilege of making our own decisions. That is the reasoning for us having a tool such as the mind which functions by thinking. However, our decisions are to be based on His Word. If you have not been taught about the Heavenly Father and His Commands, what basis does one have to form a correct opinion.

Evil is prevalent. It's possessing the world. Guns, drugs, low self esteem, poverty, sickness, and hunger are all symptoms of evil. As a matter of fact, we have a tendency to become quite defensive even questioning a good positive action. We view this behavior as not trust worthy. This reflects the direction of our minds in this world.

In the following pages, I'd like to provide you
with a few guidelines on which you can base your decision. Don't
be turned off by the Biblical Scriptures in this book, especially in the
beginning, for they are the facts of life, and they were derived from
the Word. The Word came straight from the mouth of The Almighty
Creator of everything that is. It is necessary for you to know: Whom...
What... Why... and Where... our Creator, Our Heavenly Father is. As
you continue to read your heart should open to a desire to seek more
knowledge regarding this most important matter.

Scriptures selectively listed in this book have
been taken from The New Century Version of the Holy Bible, The
Jerusalem Bible, The New International Version Bible Called Free
on the Inside, which is a prison issued Bible, The Apocrypha, and
The BOOK. The New Unger's Bible Dictionary was also a source of
reference.

The Book, which is mentioned above is not a Bible
that I've seen used as often as I would like, but I love it. It's a special
edition of The Living Bible published by Tyndale House Publishers

Inc. This particular edition is one of the easiest to understand since
it is a thought-for-thought translation. The ideas are expressed here
as ordinary people in the late twentieth century would say them
with our word--pictures and expressions. The language is not that
of the translation of the Hebrew and Greek texts which is used in
the King James Versions. Therefore, it is a great start for acquiring
understanding for the newcomer.

It's very important for you to receive this message
in your spirit, for God does Bless His children with all the good things
that their hearts desire. Learn what He's wanting to do for you, and
see if it's not more than you can do for yourself. I challenge you to put
these facts to work in your life, and behold; 'If you believe', the glory
that I speak of will manifest itself right before your eyes.

God Bless You!

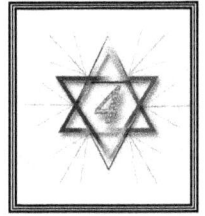

Our Father God

It's amazing but I don't know of anyone, who in a bind trying to add validity to their point, or needing help, does not call upon the name of Our Father God. "Lord help me... I swear to God... I raise my hand to God... As God is my witness... My God..." and the newest acronym "OMG", Etc., Etc., Etc..

We're quick to use His name in vain. Letting it flow from our mouths with out giving it any thought. And please let's not forget the most popular. I swear on my Mother, Father, Sister, Brother and whom ever else I feel that you may accept as being important enough for me to convince you that what I'm saying can be accepted as the truth. "My God, why am I so ..." Then comes the negative quotes; "Stupid, slow, etc." (You get the picture!)

This is a form of blasphemy committed out of ignorance through thoughtlessness, weakness of the flesh, and low self esteem. When we use phases such as these, we are actually wanting to be believed, pitied, or we're calling out for help from whomever we're speaking with. We're not confident in ourselves, nor do we really believe that God has even heard our appeal. It's just something to say. Maybe someone will fall for this, and we can get our way.

Whatever the case, we are looking to gain something by using these phrases at that time. Most of us do not realize this is a No--No. Those of us that are aware of this, don't take it seriously. Why? Because, we are more concerned with appealing to the person standing in front of our eyes than we are with Our Heavenly Father who is everywhere at once, and has the ability to remove the voice from our vocal chords in an instant. The Bible, which is the final word, instructs us: "Say just a simple "Yes, I will, or No, I won't" Your word is enough. To strengthen your promise with a vow shows that something is wrong. (Matthew 5:37 The Book)

What's worse is people that use the name of God to convince another person, whether it be truth or lie, is being disobedient. And we wonder why God doesn't bless us out of uncomfortable situations immediately. Why should he? Do we really deserve to be freed from the bondage of our own creations? Just give thanks that Our Father is a merciful God, and we have the chance to repent and correct our wrongs. He does forgive. Otherwise this earth; and everything on, around and above it would simply be a dark expanse just as it was in the beginning. I'd say that we have certainly jerked His plan totally out of proportion from His original intent. Keep reading. It will all become crystal clear.

GOD, A MAN OR A WOMAN

Our Father who reigns supreme over all, sees all-hears all, is the Beginning and the End. He is the Almighty, The God of the Universe. He Created us to be His children, and He sees all the wrong, as well as, the right that is done by us.

Common questions asked about the

personification of God are: "Where did God come from? Who created Him?" This is truly controversial. By that I mean I have actually met people who attempted to engage me in an argument as to the gender of Our God; the Creator of Heaven and Earth. I've seen banners on automobiles that indicate that God is a woman. One banner read; "God is coming, and she is Pissed." This is deception in the rawest form, no doubt perpetrated by ignorance.

> (Revelation 1:8 The Book)
> "I am the A and the Z, The Beginning and the Ending of all things." Says God, who is the Lord, the All Powerful One who is, and was, and is coming again!

Gods' Spirit has always been here, and will always be here. This was His home, even before He created it for us.

> (Genesis 1:1-2 The Amplified Bible)
> In the beginning God formed and created the heavens and the earth. The earth was without form, and an empty waste, and darkness was upon the face of the very great deep.

The Spirit of God was moving in empty space. God is a Spirit, and no where, in the Bible, does it refer to Him as 'male or female' per say. The word 'He,' that confuses the inexperienced reader of the WORD, is used in a generic sense. Whenever the sex is unspecified in any publication or speech, 'He' is the word commonly used.

A Spirit is a supernatural being or essence. Webster's Dictionary meaning of Spirit is: [An often malevolent being that is bodiless, but can become visible. It also says that malevolent means; having, showing, or arising from intense often vicious ill will, spite, or hatred.]

The Spirit of God is Holy; He is perfect, He is pure, He is love, He is also filled with supernatural and potentially fatal powers. He can transform to any form that suits His purpose. However, I prefer to think that my God is a laid back type of Spirit. He has plenty of entities in His Heavenly Court to happily carry out all of His orders and commands. He created it like that.

IN THE NAME OF GOD

The two essential and persona names of God in the Hebrew Scriptures are: ELOHIM, calling attention to the fullness of Divine Power. The second is JEHOVAH, (more correctly YAHWEH) meaning "He who is" and therefore declaring the Divine Self Existence. The names listed below are varied or combined with others to bring out or emphasize certain attributes of the Godhead.

- Jehovah - Jireh - The Lord will provide
- Jehovah - Nissi - The Lord is my banner
- Jehovah - Shalom - The Lord is Peace
- Jehozabad - (Jehovah Endowed)
- Jehovah - Shamah - The Lord is there.

The English word God is identical with the Anglo-Saxon word for 'Good', therefore, it is believed that the name God refers to the Divine Goodness. God, as revealed through the Scriptures, is the one Infinite and Eternal Being. He is Purely Spiritual; The Supreme Personal Intelligence, The Creator and Preserver of all things, The Perfect Moral Ruler of the Universe. He is the only Proper Object of worship.

THE TRINITY

Jehovah God is a tri-personal entity consisting of the Father, Son and Holy Spirit, most commonly referred to as the Trinity; Constituting one Godhead. These three are joint partakers of the same nature and majesty of God. The Trinity is one of the great mysteries of revelation because it is not understood by the human mind. In many religions that except God as the Creator, The tri-personality is not acknowledged nor accepted.

In Gods' own time Jesus, the second person of the Trinity, was sent into the world to give the Good News that Jehovah God would forgive all of our sins. He has given us His Divine protection if we would accept Jesus as our Lord and Savior: confess our sins to Jesus (not to man), and repent.

Jesus was to die and be raised up again to the Father in Heaven. In this sacrifice we became entitled to return to the coverage of His Goodness after falling from grace because of our disobedience. We who qualify for this wonderful gift believe that Jesus Christ is the only Son of God; born of virgin birth, was crucified to give satisfaction for the wrong that was done by us, and to give us the opportunity to be forgiven through acceptance of this fact. He was raised from death ascending to the right side of His, as well as Our FATHER in Heaven, thereby defeating Satan.

When Jesus was crucified, The Holy Spirit, the third person of the Trinity was released onto the earth. Though united to both in the mysterious oneness of the Godhead, The Holy Spirit is a person separate from the Father, and the Son. He is not simply a representative of a person, or a figure of speech. He is an intelligent agent possessing self consciousness and freedom. He is to be worshiped and glorified along with the Father and Son. To sin against the Holy Spirit, which is the Spirit of God, is an unpardonable sin. Jesus says in His teachings: "Even blasphemy against me or any other sin can be forgiven, all except one: Speaking against the Holy Spirit shall never be forgiven, either in this world or in the world to come." (Matthew 12:31-32 The Book)

THE POWER OF JEHOVAH GOD

God is the most High that only has to say:

"Let there be light", and there was light. (Genesis 1:3)

The Infinite Power, who can and has commanded enormously large occurrences to take place throughout the Bible such as:

- Sending rain onto the earth for forty days and forty nights. Wiping from the face of the earth every living creature that the Spirit of God had Created (Genesis 7:4)
- Raining down, out of the Heavens, burning sulfur onto Sodom and Gomorrah because of the inhabitants vile behavior. (Genesis 19:24)
- Giving Moses the ability to raise his walking stick that could have, very well, only been a reed stick taken from the Red

Sea, possessing the power that God had placed upon it, and extending it out over the sea so that the sea would separate, thereby, allowing Gods' people to cross on dry land.

God knew His people were very frightened and too mentally worn down to deal with a battle. They had been in captivity as slaves in Egypt for 400 years before their Exodus. (Exodus 14:16)

The Exodus was the great deliverance extended to the Israelites. God used Moses to bring the Sons of Israel, His Chosen People, out of the Land of Egypt with a mighty hand, and an outstretched arm. Moses, speaking to the people said,

(Exodus 14: 14 The Amplified Bible)
"The Lord will fight for you and you shall hold your peace and remain at rest."

This is an example of our awesome Father Gods' power and willingness to fight our battles if we allow Him;

(Jehovah Shamah - The Lord is There).

Many people have an attitude, and the unknowledgeable belief, that this occurred only in Biblical times. It doesn't happen like that in the 21st Century. Wrong! It does happen in these days in each of our lives when we expect it. Believing that He can, and will make great things take place in our existence is the key to seeing His marvelous works. It's called having faith in God's Word.

Our Heavenly Father is our Creator. To be more precise, God designed us; our souls which were created before He created our home; This world. Our Father performed this miracle by speaking as the Creator King announcing His crowning work to the members of the His Heavenly Court. Consider the creativity and ingenuity in building a human body that functions with power, the ability to think, be mobile, have emotions, and regenerate with a night of sleep. It was done by speaking a Word, "Let there be," and there was. God said:

(Genesis 1:26 The NIV Study Bible)
"Let us make human beings in our image and likeness,
and let them rule over the fish in the sea, and the birds
in the sky, over the tame animals, over all the earth, and
over the small crawling animals on the earth."

The plurality of the word, 'US', that God speaks of is presumed by me, as well as, The Amplified Bible to be the Trinity. (The Father, Son and The Holy Spirit) along with His many mighty

Angels.

We know, by now, that He is the God Head, The Chief, and the Man in Charge. The Son and the Holy Spirit are in Him, and have been with Him from the beginning of time. They are a part of Him. The beginning of time is forever ago. No man knows when time began. Our Father is infinity times infinity years old. Who knows when He decided to create the Human beings as we know them. The limitations of human understanding doesn't permit us to comprehend how God thinks, or how His existence came to be. God says, while communicating with Isaiah:

> (Isaiah 55:8 The NIV Study Bible)
> "For my thoughts are not your thoughts, neither are your ways my ways, "Declares the Lord.
> "As the Heavens are higher than the earth, so are my ways higher than your ways, and my thoughts, than your thoughts."

The comparison of us being created in the image of God does not mean that we have the same physical characteristics as Him; two arms, two legs, head, hands, and feet. Being created in His image refers to His Righteousness and Holiness; His Perfection and Love, but not limited to these. This was what we were created to be.

Therefore, it is in our personalities to be righteous people. However, evil is constantly attempting to dominate our minds. Because of this, we see corruption all around us as well as in us. We also have been given the trait of being potentially fatal. This characteristic exist in our minds. It can be controlled by our own will, or can be free to run rampant, thereby, staging self destruction of--or-- in our lives.

Jehovah God has brought into existence, by the free exercise of His Creative Power, the world and all orders of beings that live within it.

Psalm 33:6-11

He merely spoke, and the heavens were formed, and all the galaxies of stars.

He made the oceans, pouring them into His vast reservoir Let everyone in all the world, men, women, and children, fear the Lord and stand in awe of Him. For when He spoke, the world began! It appeared at His command! And with a breath, He can scatter the plans of all the nations who oppose Him, but His own plan stands forever. His intentions are the same for every generation.

Realize how special we are. God gave us rule over all the creatures that move along the ground, all the fish of the sea, and birds of the air. Since man is made in Gods image, every human being is worthy of honor and respect. Kingship has been given to us. When you think of yourself, do so as a child of the King. Refer to yourself as, 'The Kings' Kid,' and act accordingly.

Jehovah God has vowed never to leave his children, nor forsake them. His promise is to us, as it was our great ancestors. It will be for our children, and their children until the end of time. Therefore, do call upon the name of Our Father God. Without shame, lift your hands high extending the palms and fingers upward towards the Heavens. Give Thanks and Praises, as well as to ask the Lord's Forgiveness for your sins. Believe that you will receive when you pray, and you will be blessed. He has the Power to make all things possible. But we must live in expectancy to see them come to pass.

OUR FATHER AND MUSIC

(Psalm 33:1-3 The BOOK)
Let all the joys of the godly well up in praise to the
LORD, for it is right to praise Him.
Play joyous melodies of praise upon the lyre and on the
harp.
Compose new songs of praise to Him, accompanied
skillfully on the harp; sing joyfully.

Instrumental music, as well as vocal music was common in ancient Israel. King Saul was influenced by it. David, before being appointed by God as King over Israel, played skillfully upon the lyre for King Saul. It had a profound effect upon Saul when he was fill with the tormenting spirit that gorged him with depression and fear. This spirit was sent upon him by Jehovah because of his disobedience.

(1 Samuel 16:23 The BOOK)
And whenever the tormenting spirit from God troubled Saul, David would play the harp and Saul would feel better, and the evil spirit would go away.

King Saul, the first King appointed by God to the Israelites defied the command of God, and God used His Fatal Power to punished Saul. God also allowed Saul's spirit to be soothed by David's musical ability.

Although, praying to Jehovah about a bothersome situation as a way of relief from it, the answer does not always come as quickly as we would like. I am by no means inferring that the Lord does not answer our prayers immediately, but it is clear to me that He does not always respond in a way that is visible for my eyes to feast upon, and get satisfaction quickly. If a condition of low spirits persist in me, regardless of what has caused them, I will immediately pop a Spiritual CD into the stereo and pump-up the Praise music. Dancing and singing along, while raising my hands to God is a guaranteed antidote for my downtrodden spirits. Praise music removes from my mind the plaguing of my own dire circumstances, and replaces it with how great and capable Our Father God is. Also it pleases Jehovah to be worshiped in this manner.

Think of some of the lyrics to music today. To be more precise, Rap music. It is so disliked by the spiritually enlightened generation because of the offensiveness of the words. It offers a negative message for the most part. We must take into consideration that the young people are singing about what they know: Guns, violence, killing, sex in the lowest level of obscenity, and police brutality.

Rap means to 'talk'. Talking about something positive would certainly be more acceptable. I'm sure Our Father would be greater pleased with this approach. After all the Scriptures says, "Sing to the Lord a new song." Rap can be considered a new way of projecting music. Once again, let me say, If you don't know the Father and what He expects from you, then there is no way to know how to please Him. What would please the Lord is to Bless Him at all times, and continually let your Praises be in the lyrics to go forth into His Universe.

As a religious ceremony, vocal music first appears in the book of Exodus. Miriam, Moses sister, in celebration of the Israelites miraculous passage through the Red Sea, led a performance of two alternating groups singing Praises to the Lord. The Lyrics of this first known rap song, as I refer to it, can be found in the book of Exodus 15:1-21. It recites the powers of Jehovah-Shamah (The Lord is There) and how they saw His amazing works being performed. The people sang to the Lord gloriously because of the triumph that He'd given to them. It was a Happy Day for those who had been in bondage by the Egyptians.

Because of the disobedience of the Jews to

Jehovah's Commands, He did not block the Egyptians from taking them into slavery. During their 400 years in captivity, they were given the lowly backbreaking jobs of brick making. They were responsible for the building of the great Tombs and Pyramids in Egypt that remain standing even until this day. Even as slaves, the blessings of their talents and skills remained with them. When ever possible they sang praises to Jehovah (Yahweh) in spite of their situation.

In the last days of Moses' life, God knowing that the people were going to return to evil, instructed Moses to give a message to the Jews. Moses did so in, what can be considered, a form of rap singing which is in the book of Deuteronomy 32:1-47. I call this rap because it was a message that was given. That is, in fact, what rapping is. When I read Miriam and Moses song, I was amazed. If I didn't know better, I would think some of the rap singers are trying to imitate Gods' awesomeness. How can this be? Have they read this portion of the Bible? There is something very profound to be said about what we think is new.

Ecclesiastes 1:9-11 The Book
History merely repeats itself. Nothing is truly new; it has all been done or said before. What can you point to that is new? How do you know it didn't exist ages ago? We don't remember what happened in those

former times, and in the future generations, no one will remember what we have done back here.

We have lyrics describing drive by shooting's, as well as, many other negative lyrics as though it's an okay thing to do. Not one person entertaining the thoughts that come across in rap music can contribute anything of worth to the Divine Creation. "JUST SAY NO', to lyrics of today's music that infiltrate your brain waves with negativity. The subliminal message is damaging. It's propagated by evil, and totally against that which God desires for His Creation.

The devil in these cases are the people in the recording industries who are in position to make decisions regarding what the lyrics to the rap music should say. Those people that convince our young desperate rappers, eager to experience success, that they can only be signed to a contract to produce their work if they sing about violence. These CEO devils that run the recording business' make every attempt to assure, the eagerly yearning to be stars, that this is what the fans want. The Rap entertainers immediately fall into their traps, because they feel this is their only chance for being triumphant. They simply sell out for what can be seen. This is only because they don't know any better. Many of them find that they are soon swallowed up by those same demons. The devil gets richer while the artist wound up back on the streets where they came from.

There are varieties of styles in Spiritual music just as there are in worldly music. It would be best to choose lyrics that help to raise our level of faith, not those which infest our minds when we look upon the terrible situation that we may find ourselves in. Discover your style. One that offer words that build strength when you are weak, and bring some relief into your life.

JEHOVAH COMMANDS US TO LOVE

The Lord God does have a very important command that we are expected to be obedient to. As was asked of Jesus by the Sadducees, and answered by Jesus in, (Mark 12:29-31 The NIV Study Bible)

"The most important command is this. The Lord Our God is the only Lord. Love the Lord your God with all your heart, all your soul, all your mind, and all your strength. The second command is this: Love your neighbor, as you love yourself. There are no commands more important than these."

There is not enough emphasis put on love in this world despite what Our Father God commands of us. It's given with conditions by most of us. We love our family members, mother, father, sister, brother, spouse, fiancé, our children, and very few others. We've learned that the greatest command is love because God is Love. Imagine if we possessed the love for each other that He has for us.

One does not think of harming a loved one, nor stealing from them. We would not establish intimate personal relationships with anyone else's husbands, or wives unless the evil spirit was within us. We would not shoot them, give or sell drugs to them, and leave them homeless not extending our hospitality. Having a loving heart would not allow us to feel comfortable doing these things. It's how we've been created. This alone could make a drastic change in the world, but we are on a destructive path. We are rebelling against the holiness and righteousness that we were created to be, and to express the goodness which has been created within us.

Just know that although we, seemingly, get by sometimes for a very long time, nothing that we do is a secret to God.

Something to consider is that we can be eliminated in a flash. Our air supply can be terminated with God simply speaking the Word. Just sitting down here chillin--all absorbed in our worldly belongings, and poof, we're all gone.. We certainly underestimated the power that God possesses. We take His love and compassion for granted. At some point we will have to answer for our every action. However, it's not too late to get right with God; For our Father God sent the Savior; the Redeemer of lost mankind. Lost meaning being without God in our lives, or purpose and hope in the Spirit of God.

MESSIAH - MESSENGER - SON OF MAN - THE WORD

This is the mystery that baffles people who are not informed. Even though I spoke of the Trinity previously in this chapter, I would like to expound on this subject a bit more. Jesus, The WORD made flesh, was in fact God himself, as well as, the fact that He was a separate person in the form of man while here on earth. The Holy Spirit is God himself even though he is an individual as well. Each has their own particular function, but they answer to the one Godhead which is the Almighty.

Please understand, this is not your next door neighbor, whom you see coming and going, and you are now able to predict their next move. This also dispels the notion that we humans are created in the same physical body form as God. I'm not aware of any human having three distinctive physical characters within one body. Each having it's own job to perform. One part laying down His life to save others. Another part giving comfort, instruction, and guidance, and both answering to the one head while still being separated to do their jobs, but united as one. Is this not a mystery that is impossible to be perceived with the natural mind?

God gave all Humans a brain to process decisions. Originally, our thoughts would have automatically been influenced by that which is in the same image of God. That image encompasses His righteousness, His love, His compassion. Though it is said, "People only use ten percent of their brain capacity." I say to you, "If you used one hundred percent of it; straining to the maximum, you would not be able to figure God, and how He is so capable to do the things that He does."

We should try to properly understand, even though we can not mentally grasp, the divine personality of God. It should not hinder our acknowledgment and acceptance of the atonement which made it possible for our sins to be washed away forever. With that in mind, let me introduce you to Jesus.

The Virgin Mary; mother of Jesus, after being told she would give birth to a child, ask, "But how can I have a baby? I am a virgin." The Angel replied, "The Holy Spirit shall come upon you, and the power of God shall overshadow you; so the baby born to you will be utterly Holy, the Son of God."

(Luke 1:34 The NIV Study Bible).

Christ, the official title of Jesus, means the Anointed One. The Messiah, which is the Messenger, and the Christ of the Scriptures, met and united themselves together in the personality of Jesus who was anointed of God as the Prophet, Priest and King. When we pray to Jehovah, we are to do so through Jesus. It was Jesus, whom through the sacrifice of Himself while here on earth, made it possible for Father God to receive us again.

Christ Jesus described as the Son of Man was relating to Our Father God using the blood line of King David's descendants, Mary and Joseph, in which to manifest Christ into human form through immaculate conception. Jesus was best known by His followers in His human form. He was the seed, the perfect man planted in this world to deliver the Good News. He was a sinless man in sinful flesh. He himself never committed a sin.

As the Son of God, He was the miracle worker, the healer. He is related to and reigned with the Father in Heaven even before this world existed. The proof of this was with the baptism by John the Baptist.

(Matthew 3:16-17) (Act 10:38 The Book)
As soon as Jesus came up out of the water, the Heavens were opened to him, and he saw the Spirit of God coming down in the form of a dove. And a voice from Heaven said, "This is my beloved Son, and I am wonderfully pleased with him."
And you, no doubt, know that Jesus of Nazareth was anointed by God with the Holy spirit and with power, and He went around doing good and healing all who

were possessed by demons, for God was with Him.

Other miracles involved His bringing back to life those who had died, healing those who were incurable, and giving hope to those who were lost.

(Matthew 11:28-30 NIV)
"Come to me, all of you who are tired and have heavy loads and I will give you rest.
Accept my teachings and learn from me, because I am gentle and humble in spirit, and you will find rest for your lives.
The teaching that I ask you to adopt is easy; the load I give you to carry is light."
The light load that Jesus speaks of is believing that he will do what He says he'll do, and for us to follow His Commandments.

(John 1:14 The Book)
Christ Jesus was the Word, in human form. The Word became a human, and lived among us.
We saw his glory, the glory that belongs to the only Son of the Father, and He was full of grace and truth.
At the name of Jesus every knee should bow of those who are in Heaven, and on earth, and every tongue should confess that Jesus Christ is Lord to the Glory of

God the Father.

Jesus Commandments, in a nutshell, is to love one another as was instructed by the Almighty. With love in our hearts, we are guided away from doing evil. The load that we give to Jesus are the pressures of this world. We are to give them to Him, and be patient allowing Him to take care of them. As noncomplex as this sounds, it isn't as simple when you are in a worldly frame of mind.

We have a tendency to pray for a change, especially in crisis type situations. When we don't see the Lord working on it fast enough, we snatch it back. Sometimes we feel we've now come up with an idea that will get us gratification. However, for some reason the problem still persist, or we've gotten ourselves into worse trouble by trying to take vengeance into our own hands, or executing a plan that has not been blessed by God. In this act, we either feel that Our Father God does not deem us worthy enough to waste His time rescuing us, or He hasn't heard us. Wrong on both counts! This is my opinion. "In the plan that God has for each of our lives, there is a preparation period. Though, He does hear our prayers, the timing may not coincide with His plans. Realize also we will experience trials and tribulations. Even a baby has to crawl before they walk, and when they finally begin to walk they fall quite often before they master the art of stepping. One must also consider the fact that they are committing a sin by not trusting Our Creator."

Believing and following the Word of Jehovah is vital. He does give us the opportunity to apologize to Him through repentance. However, you can not repeat the same sinful actions over and over again and continuously ask for forgiveness. There are consequences that you will pay. The Father will give you a good spanking, and you won't have any choice but too accept it, because you can not run and hide. What's reassuring is Father God loves His children even when administering punishment. On the other hand, you can continue following the ways of the world, and receive unbearable punishment. Think about that.

It is a known fact that what goes around comes around. It is always much easier to do evil deeds to others, than to receive someone doing evil to you. With this knowledge you can assess your alternatives. Life has a way of catching up with us, and beating us down to a point of calling on somebody for help. I am not speaking of financial help, because having finances doesn't cover everything. You'll always need more than money. You'll need the

Super Natural Power of the Heavenly Father to come into your life, and rescue you from circumstances that you probably created for yourself.

We have a way of blaming Satan for all our problems: Satan caused our health to fail, or Satan caused us to lose everything that we've acquired. How many people did we extend our time, finances, or whatever would be of assistance when they needed help. As God Blesses us, we are to be a Blessing to others. As I said previously, "What goes around, comes around." I rest my case on this issue.

HOLY SPIRIT - HOLY GHOST -
SPIRIT OF GOD

Jesus said, "If you love me, obey me; and I will ask the Father, and He will give you another Comforter, and He will never leave you. He is the Holy Spirit, the Spirit who leads into all truth. The world at large can not receive Him, for it isn't looking for Him and doesn't recognize Him. But you do, for He lives with you now, and someday shall be in you." (John 14:15-16)

Holy Spirit, Holy Ghost, Spirit of God are all the same personification with different names. Most people are not aware of the importance of the Holy Spirit, and His function in the Believers life. He, 'not It', is God just as Jesus is God. Take notice that He is not an 'It'.

Although it is easier for the babe in Christianity to relate to Jesus because of the facts they've read in the Scriptures; that He walked on this earth in human form just as we do, the job of the Holy Spirit is equally as important. The Holy Ghost is a free agent possessing intelligence and freedom. He decides when to stay or leave.

The Holy Spirit of God walks with the believers. His job is to instruct, sanctify, comfort and regenerate those who believe, and have accepted Christ putting forth an effort to grow their faith in God. He performs His job quite amazingly, I must say.

I've had to call on Him on numerous occasions when times have presented situations that would have caused me to explode causing Hell to come up to this level, as if Hell is not already on this level. The Spirit of God would noticeable intercede upon my calling His name. I know that His Spirit will not contend with confusion, therefore, I have had to make an extra effort to refrain from causing Him to freely walk away on occasions. This is not the only area He has functioned perfectly in my life. He has been with me throughout the writing of this book, in which I am truly grateful and thankful knowing that I could not do this without Him.

Many have personally experienced the sensation of being filled with the Joy of The Holy Spirit. It is as if one has a halo glowing over their head; an illuminating light that draws good and bad people to you, but only desiring, conscientiously or unconsciously, to say and do good things for you.

The positivism that develops in ones' personality through faith in the Word of The Heavenly Father begins on the inside and projects outwardly. You cease to fight with the world for survival because you know that Our Lord Christ Jesus has won the ultimate battle when He laid down His life so that our sins would be erased. He rose from the dead three days later to ascend into Heaven. Our Lord now exalts on the right hand side of Our Father God. Upon Our Lord Jesus arrival back to His Heavenly reign, the Father of All Creation released His Holy Spirit to guide us in our walk with Him. Believing and accepting this fact restores our position as a King's Kid.

HE GAVE HIS LIFE FOR OUR SALVATION

Romans 5:6-8 THE BOOK
Your old evil desires were nailed to the cross with him;
that part of you that loves to sin was crushed and fatally
wounded so that your sin-loving body is no longer
under sin's control; no longer needs to be a slave to sin,
for when you are deadened to sin you are freed from all
it's allure and its power over you.

To confess the acceptance of Christ Jesus with our mouths is our first step towards being saved. We must realize the purpose in which Jesus was sent down from His Heavenly position to live among us in the form of flesh the same as ours. The sacrifice of God's only begotten son, the suffering, the shedding of His blood, and the ultimate, the crucifixion were the only way that God could forgive mankind for turning away from Him. This was the atonement designed by God to meet His satisfaction that would allow the doors to be reopened for the human race to reunite with Him. This includes all Humans regardless of the color of their skin, the size of their nose, or the country that they are from.

At this point, which is approaching the closing of this chapter, I would be remiss to not include an opportunity for you to accept Christ Jesus into you life if you have not already done so.

By reading the upcoming confession, you will reunite your Soul with Jehovah (Yahweh). You will then receive the Holy Spirit into your life. He will do all, that Christ Jesus said, for you. You will experience a change in how you think about things. Slowly but surely, if you truly believe, your life will transform as you begin to experience a more positive frame of mind.

A PRAYER OF SALVATION:

LORD JESUS, I want you to come into my life right now.

I am a sinner.

I have been trusting in myself, and in my own works,

But now I put my trust in you.

I accept you as my own personal Savior.

I believe that you died for me.

I receive you as the Lord and Master, over my life.

Help me to turn from my sins, and follow you.

I accept your gift of eternal life.

I am not worthy of it Jehovah God,

But I thank you for sending Your Holy Spirit into my life,

and for letting me be born again.

Amen; And So It Is

At this point experience freedom. Take a deep

breath and give Praise to the Lord. You have just aligned yourself with Our Creator--The Almighty. You will now make a consciences effort, not to continue to sin. You will enjoy the peace that the Blood of Jesus has entitled you too. You will tell someone, right now, that you have been set free, and that you have received Salvation by accepting Christ Jesus as your personal Lord and Savior. God will truly Bless You.

THE SONG OF MOSES

The people of Israel sang this Song to the Lord in celebration
of their deliverance from Egypt and Pharaoh.

I will sing to the Lord,
for He has triumphed gloriously;
He has thrown both horse and rider into the sea.
The lord is my strength,
My song and my salvation.
He is my God, and I will praise Him.
He is my Father's God--I will exalt Him.
The Lord is a warrior,
Yes, Jehovah is His name.
He has overthrown Pharaoh's Chariots and Armies,

Drowning them in the sea.

The famous Egyptian Captains

are dead beneath the waves.

The water covers them.

They went down into the depths like a stone.

Your right hand, O Lord, is glorious in power;

It dashes the enemy to pieces.

In the greatness of your Majesty,

You overthrew all those who rose against you.

You sent forth your anger,

and it consumed them as fire consumes straw.

At the blast of your breath the waters divided!

They stood as solid walls to hold the seas apart.

The enemy said, "I will chase after them,"

Catch up with them, destroy them.

I will cut them apart with my sword,

and divide the captured booty."

But God blew with His wind, and sea covered them.

They sank as lead in the mighty waters.

Who else is like the Lord among the Gods?

You have led the people you redeemed.

But in your loving - kindness,

You have guided them wonderfully, to your Holy Land.

The Nations heard what happened, and they trembled.

Fear has gripped the people of Philistia.

The leaders of Edom, are appalled.

The mighty men of Moab, tremble;

All the people of Canaan, melt with fear.

Terror and dread have overcome them.

O Lord, because of your great power, they won't attack us!

We'll pass by them in safety.

You will bring them in,

and plant them on your mountain,

Your own homeland, Lord,

The sanctuary you made them to live in.

Jehovah shall reign forever and forever.

The horses of Pharaoh, his Horsemen,

and his Chariots, tried to follow through the sea;

But the Lord let down the wall of water on them

while the people of Israel walked through on dry land.

Then Miriam the Prophetess, the sister of Aaron, took a tambourine

and led the women in dances.

Miriam sang this song:

Sing to the Lord for he has triumphed gloriously.

The horse and rider have been drowned in the sea.

MOSES' SONG Deuteronomy 32:1-47

"Listen, O heavens and earth!

Listen to what I say!

My words shall fall upon you,

Like the gentle rain and dew,

Like rain upon the tender grass,

Like showers on the hillside.

I will proclaim the greatness of the Lord.

His work is perfect.

How glorious He is! He is the Rock.

Everything He does is just and fair.

He is faithful, without sin.

But Israel has become corrupt,

Smeared with sin.

They are no longer His;

They are a stubborn, twisted generation.

Is this the way you treat Jehovah?

O foolish people,

Is not God your Father?

Has He not established you and made you strong?

Remember the days of long ago!

Ask your father and the aged men,

They will tell you all about it.

When God divided up the world among the nations.

He gave each of them a supervising Angel!

But He appointed none for Israel;

For Israel was God's own personal possession!

God protected them in the howling wilderness,

As though they were the apple of His eye.

He spreads His wings over them,

Even as an eagle over spreads her young.

She carries them upon her wings, As does the Lord, His people!

When the Lord alone was leading them,

And they lived without foreign gods,

God gave them fertile hilltops, rolling, fertile fields,

Honey from the rock, And olive oil from stony ground!

He gave them milk and meat,

Choice Bashan Rams, and goats,

And the finest of the wheat;

They drank the sparkling wine, But Israel was soon over fed;

Yes, fat and bloated;

Then, in plenty, they forsook their God.

They shrugged away the Rock of their Salvation.

Israel began to follow foreign gods, An Jehovah was very angry;

He was jealous of His people.

They sacrificed to heathen gods,

To new gods never before worshipped.

They spurned the Rock who had made them,

Forgetting it was God who had given them birth.

God saw what they were doing,

And detested them!

His sons and daughters were insulting him.

He said, 'I will abandon them then!

For they are a stubborn, faithless generation.

They have made me very jealous of their idols,

Which are not gods at all.

Now I, in turn, will make them jealous

By giving my affections

To the foolish Gentile nations of the world.

For my anger has kindled a fire

that burns to the depths of the underworld,

consuming the earth and all of its crops,

and setting its mountains on fire.

I will waste them with hunger,

burning fever, and fatal disease.

I will devour them! I will set wild beasts upon them,

to rip them apart with their teeth;

And deadly serpents, crawling in the dust.

Outside, the enemies sword;

Inside, the Plague shall terrorize young men and girls alike;

The baby nursing at the breast, and the aged men.

I had decided to scatter them to distant lands,

so that even the memory of them would disappear,

but then I thought, "My enemies will boast,

"Israel is destroyed by our own might;

It was not the Lord who did it!'"

Israel is a stupid nation;

Foolish, without understanding.

Oh, that they were wise!' Oh, that they could understand!

Oh, that they would know what they are getting into!

How could one single enemy chase a thousand of them,

and two put ten thousand to flight,

unless their Rock had abandoned them,

unless the Lord had destroyed them?

But the rock of other nations,

is not like our Rock'

Prayers to their gods are valueless.

They act like men of Sodom and Gomorrah;

Their deeds are bitter with poison;

They drink the wine of serpent venom.

but Israel is my special people,

sealed as jewels within my treasury.

vengeance is mine,

and I decree the punishment of all her enemies:

Their doom is sealed. The Lord will see his people righted, and will have compassion on them when they slip.

He will watch their power ebb away,

both slave and free.

Then God will ask, "Where are their gods,

The rocks they claimed to be their refuge?

Where are these gods now,

to whom they sacrificed their fat and wine?

Let those gods arise, and help them!

Don't you see that I alone am God?

I kill and make live; I wound and heal,

no one delivers from my power.

I raise my hand to heaven, and vow by my existence,

that I will whet the lighting of My sword!

and hurl my punishments upon my enemies!

My arrows shall be drunk with blood!

My sword devours the flesh and blood of all the slain and captives.

The heads of the enemy are gory with blood.'

Praise His people, Gentile nations,

for He will avenge His people;

Taking vengeance on His enemies,

purifying His land and His people."

When Moses and Joshua had recited all the words
of this song to the people, Moses made these comments:

"Meditate upon all the laws I have given you today, and pass them on to your children. These laws are not mere words, they are your life! Through obeying them you will live long, plentiful lives in the land you are going to possess across the Jordan River."

The Will of God; His Commands and Laws are found throughout the book of Deuteronomy. It would behoove you to read what He requires of His Creation, and what the rewards for obedience are.

SALVATION

It's hard for me to describe, without becoming emotional, how profound the benefit of Salvation is. It is the greatest gift ever given to all mankind. It separates us from the world, and places us in position to receive all that has been created by God for us. It once in for all establishes our superiority. Because of what one man gave of himself, this entire creation has an opportunity that many can not phantom. The Heavens has been opened to send down the desires of our hearts. All that we have done against the Will of our Creator is able to be washed away without a thought of it ever being brought back to mind.

The fullness of love has been extended to us

through the Blood that was shed to remove the evils from our hearts, and for our minds to be opened to the greatness that we were created to be. All things can be overcome because of the Blood that poured from the wounds of the whip stripes viciously laid upon the body of Jesus; The only begotten Son of God.

As he bore the lashing of the leather steel tipped whip, the beatings from the hands of other men, the degradation and humiliation, He was a man like any other that walked this earth. He stood between us, and our eternal damnation caused by our sinful ways. He was blameless in every way; one who had never committed a sin. No wrong doing could ever be attributed to him. Yet, He sacrifice himself to the harshness that man can put upon another man.

I have just referred to Jesus as a man; the one that shed his Blood to save us. As He walked this earth, He did so in human flesh, with the same frailty that all humans possess. There was no unique power placed on him to block him from feeling the pain exactly as you or I would feel it. Although he was a man here on earth, He was also the Messiah sent to deliver mankind from the bondage of their creation. A Prophet to give revelation of the love of God and His intentions. A Teacher to instruct mankind how to live a purposeful life. The Christ; anointed of God to deliver the Good

News. As the 2nd part of the Trinity that answers to the Godhead, He

is God, The Redeemer of mankind, Our Savior.

Despite all of these prestigious titles, he sacrificed

himself for people that were [not even worthy to carry his sandals].

(Matthew 3:11) The extent of his sacrifice was one that no human

could withstand. Jesus did it as a man on a mission to restore his

fathers world. A world that had gone terribly wrong.

Isaiah 52:15

They shall see my Servant beaten and bloodied, so

disfigured one would scarcely know it was a person

standing there. So shall he cleanse many nations.

In his act, we have been set free from all the

negativity that plunders our lives on a daily basis.

2 Corinthians 5:21

For God took the sinless Christ and poured into him

our sins. Then, in exchange, he poured God's goodness

into us!

Isaiah 53:10

Yet it was the Lord's good plan to bruise him and fill

him with grief. But when his soul has been made

an offering for sin, then he shall have a multitude of children, many heirs. He shall live again, and God's program shall prosper in His hands.

Our Father God planned for Christ Jesus, who is in fact God Himself in part, to live among us in flesh, and to prove to us, through miracles and wonders, that He is the Son of the Living God. Christ, the Anointed One, knew in advance that He Himself would be the sacrifice, the atonement; that through His submission to being crucified, would enable Jehovah God to forgive us for all of our sins.

Jehovah God loves us to the point that even though we fought against Him, if we accept Christ Jesus as the Son of God, we are forgiven and are Saved from this world that is ruled by evil. As believers in Christ, we have received Salvation from Our Creator, and are now in line to receive all that He promises His Children.

Jesus sacrifice cleansed many nations and their people. As a matter of fact, every whip lash that cut into His flesh removed another one of our sins, and offered us complete healing. This healing encompasses every aspect of our lives. Healing of our health; our financial situation, our relationships, our decision making process, and any other thing that is not operating in the way that God created us to live, are covered under the Blood of Jesus. The Blood itself is the power that will make our lives right with God, and good for us.

Because of the Blood, we have been freed to call upon our Heavenly Father through the name of Jesus. The acceptance of the sacrifice that Jesus made became a weapon for us to use to fight against the evils of this world; God's Word is our Armor. Speaking it into our circumstances will bring about change. To not take advantage of this privilege is to cause unnecessary grief in our lives.

Telephoning a friend and a Sister in Christ; hearing the most depressed hello that you can imagine, and being very much alarmed because of the tone of her voice,

>I asked, "What's wrong?"
>"I'm not feeling well. "She muttered in a tone pitch just above a whisper.
>"What's bothering you?" I continued as I pressed the phone receiver tightly against my ear in an attempt to close out the surrounding sounds.

She mumbled something which I didn't understand. Knowing that she was attending school to be a nurse, and my hardly being able to hear her voice, I assumed she had given me some medical terminology for what was happening in her body. Replying that I didn't understand what she had said. I asked her to explain it to me in layman's language.

"I don't understand the technical terms that you're using."

"I have a blood clot in my tube." She said.

Taking a moment to digest what she said, and knowing she knows Jesus, I had to quickly censor my words. My thoughts were, "How can she lay there and let the devil tamper with her mind, and claim sickness."

My natural instinct sent me into the 'Bind Satan' frame of mind. This was one of my strong periods. I had been studying the Word all day causing my sensitivity and understanding to be extremely perceptive. Because of this, I adamantly replied,

"I don't have to tell you that by the stripes that Jesus took to His body, we are healed. You must believe that, and say it."

I could hear an eerie silence that caused me to, now, go into defense mode. I knew I had to proceed using a great deal of tack. It has been my experience that when one receives bad news, they immediately go into depression. Some will let that depression totally take over their lives transforming them into hopeless creatures.

I felt that happening through phone.

"Oops!" I whispered under my breath. "Oh well, you can't stop now."

Taking a deep breath, I proceeded.

"You know that Our Lord sustained a lot to free us from the bondage of evil. Included in that was any sickness put upon us from the devil. You declared your walk with God, now stand on His Word. By the stripes that Jesus took, I am healed. Say it!"

She repeated after me; raising her voice to the normal level. I felt a compulsion to pray for her, but instead, knowing that her mother was a Godly woman, and I didn't want to give the impression that my prayers would reached the ears of God before her Mother's did, I asked,

" Have your Mom prayed for you?"

"Yes, she has." She muttered.

"Good! You'll be fine."

Needless to say, she was fine. The cause of her trauma was the fact that she let a situation become so stressful until it affected her body.

Once we declare our acceptance of God's atonement; the sacrifice of God's only Son, and why it was that He would allow Himself to go through such a horrendous experience for a bunch of worthless people. We have to use the Armor, and stand on the Word. You don't just say, "I accept Jesus", and then revert back to hopelessness because of a message from the world.

FIRST IS JESUS

There are religions that pray to man made statues that are representative of supposedly saints. There are religious groups that hold rats in godly positions, as well as other countries that worship the elephants being the god. There are countries today, that will not acknowledge Jesus as being the Son of God. They accept him only as a prophet sent by God whom they call Allah. They persecute Christians because of their personal beliefs and acceptance of Christ. In many cases those believers are tortured violently, even in these times. All of these are wrong. There is only one Creator of Heaven and Earth. There is only one Son who sacrificed Himself to be crucified as an atonement to redeem Gods' creation of mankind. There is only one Holy Ghost that enters the body of everyone one that accepts Christ Jesus, and believes that He is the Son of God. The only way that you can be saved from your sins, and be accepted back to qualify for God's Kingdom is through the acceptance of Christ Jesus.

THE WORLDS POINT OF VIEW

People of the world, (those who have not accepted Christ as their Savior and live by their own rules), have great difficulty coming to God and allowing Jesus into their lives. Unfortunately, most of us are taught from childhood to build, and then lean on our man made crutches. This includes, but are not limited to our jobs, money, and connections. We allow ourselves to rely on these perishable things. This is our security blanket; Our ability to talk our way into, and out of situations. However, a time always comes in ones' life when all human resources fail. That's when, even nonbelievers in Christ; unaware of the benefits of the walk, sometimes call on the name of Jesus with no knowledge of why they are calling Him, or what He will do for them. Many will summon Jesus with no belief that He'll ever hear them. Some just do it to impress whomever may be listening. The last group always baffles me, because they come across so very transparent. They're Wishy Washy Christians. Boarder Liners -- Walk with Jesus when it's convenient.

Praying, reading the Word of God, and asking for clarification from the Holy Spirit is so easy to do. It also adds assurance that what you're asking for will come to pass.

Included with the proverbial security blanket that we set up for ourselves on our priority list, some of us acknowledge God whom we may place high up on it. He, in some cases is actually placed in a fluctuating position. As unacceptable as it may appear to the worldly mind, the order is as thus:

- Our Father God, Jehovah (Yahweh) who created us which includes Christ Jesus and the Holy Spirit.
- Ourselves.
- Our companions in Holy Matrimony, Husbands or Wives.
- Our children whom God have blessed us with to, raise and teach His Commands too.

There is never to be a deviation of Our Father Gods' position in our lives. Also there is still a point that we cannot get around; The fact that trust and belief in the Word of God is the motivational factor in which He operates. Our Father God saves us, and His salvation is freely given to all men, but is conditioned upon:

- Belief in Christ Jesus
- Repenting --Asking forgiveness for all the wrong things that we have done against the Will of God
- Faith that the Word of God is alive.

Walking with Christ Jesus is a daily adventure. Loving the Lord, and wanting to follow His Commands is not the most accepted path that one can take. Just as Christ Jesus was persecuted for submitting Himself for our redemption, so will we be criticized, mocked, and treated as strange birds for honoring His sacrifice. Be not dismayed though, because your reward will be great here on earth, as well as, in Heaven.

> Matthew 5:11-12 The NIV Bible
> Blessed are you when people insult you, persecute you, and falsely say all kinds of evil against you because of me.
> Rejoice and be glad, because great is your reward in Heaven, for in the same way, they persecuted the prophets who were before you.

> John 15:23-25 The NIV Bible
> He who hates me, hates my Father as well. If I had not done among them what no one else did, they would not be guilty of sin.
>
> But now they have seen these miracles, and still they have hated both me, and my father. But this is to fulfill what is written in the Law: 'They hated me without reason.'

People will dislike you because of the calmness, secure feeling, and confidence level that projects from those who have accepted Christ Jesus as their Lord and Savior. There is a difference in the personality of a person that seek to follow the Will of God, and will not be swayed by the forces of this world. The true Believer chooses God, and does not waiver based on popular opinions. The choice to be made is easy when we really consider what God did for us.

> John 3:16-21 The BOOK
> For God loved the world so much that he gave his only Son, so that anyone who believes in him, shall not perish but have eternal life. God did not send his Son into the world to condemn it, but to save it. There is no eternal doom awaiting those who trust him to save them. But those who don't trust him have already been tried and condemned for not believing in the only Son of God.
>
> Their sentence is based on this fact: that the Light from Heaven came into the world, but they loved the darkness more than the Light, for their deeds were evil. They hated the heavenly Light because they wanted to sin in the darkness. They stayed away from that Light for fear their sins would be exposed, and they would be punished. But those doing right come gladly to the Light to let everyone see that they are doing what God wants them to do.
>
> Hebrews 1:3 The BOOK

Gods Son shines out with Gods Glory, and all Gods
Son is and does marks him as God. He regulates the
universe by the mighty power of his command. He is
the one who died to cleanse us and clear our record of
all sin, and then sat down in highest honor beside the
great God of Heaven.

Psalm 27:1-3 The BOOK
The Lord is my light and my salvation: He protects me
from danger--whom shall I fear? When evil men come
to destroy me, they will stumble and fall!

PERSONALIZING YOUR PRAYERS

The average person who has relied on his own
resources for his or her entire life, find it very difficult to look to the
unseen. Many people do not get a clear understanding of the Bible
Scriptures, therefore, they don't feel they'll help them.

I suggest asking in prayer for wisdom and
understanding, each time, before reading the Scriptures. I also
recommend purchasing a New International Version (NIV) Study
Bible or the New Century Version of the Holy Bible. These two
books, along with sincere prayer, helped the magic of the Scriptures
come off the pages and into my heart. Of course back to back trials

and tribulations had me screaming for help. That stimulated the motivational force to cause me to want those doors to be opened welcoming Salvation.

There is an old spiritual hymn that says, "The Lord may not come when you call Him, but He's always on time." If you feel he isn't coming when you call, you must be patient, and not give up. Our God is very mysterious. His ways of doing things are unexplainable. We don't always know what the plan is. Sometimes it's not always what we asked for or expected. But then we are surprised with something much better than what we were asking for, especially when we don't put time limits on God.

We have all been created differently. God has a particular plan for each individual. Just because it does not appear as though He's responding doesn't mean that we should lose faith. This is the perfect time to show endurance in your faith.

This is a truly fulfilling section on being Saved, and the enormous blessings that one receives when they open their hearts to the Spirit of God. You'll find that if you place your name in the first person category denoted by a line, you can feel the Spirit of God moving in you as you read out loud. You'll begin to feel the positive power purging in your heart.

Psalm 40:1-5

I,_____, waited patiently for God to help me; then he listened and heard my cry. He lifted me out of the pit of despair; out from the bog and the mire. He set my feet on a hard firm path, and steadied me as I walked along. He has given me a new song to sing of praises to our God. Now many will hear of the glorious things he did for me, and stand in awe before the Lord, and put their trust in him. Many blessings are given to those who trust the Lord and have no confidence in those who are proud, or who trust in idols.

I ask the Lord for protection in everything I do. I pray for His Grace and Mercy every morning, and thank Him every evening.

Heavenly Father, in the name of Jesus, bless the _____family with a safe day. Dispatch the Angels that you have selected to guard us. Direct us so that we may fulfill the purpose that you have planned for us in this day. Give us strength and endurance so that we will not tire out before the job is done. We long to please you Lord, and pray that you bless us according to the faith that you have placed within our hearts, and the diligence we have put forth to

increase it.
                    In Jesus name, I pray.

                    Amen...And so it is

                    Psalms 91:1-16

I live within the shadow of the Almighty, shel-
tered by the God who is above all gods. This
I,_____, declare, that he alone
is my refuge, my place of safety; He is my god, and I,
_____,am trusting him. For he rescues
me from every trap, and protects me from the fatal
plague. He will shield me with his wings! They will
shelter me. His faithful promises are my armor. Now I
don't need to be afraid of the dark anymore, nor fear the
dangers of the day; nor dread the plagues of darkness,
nor disasters in the morning. Though a thousand fall at
my side, though ten thousand are dying around me, the
evil will not touch me. I, _____,will see how
the wicked are punished, but I will not share it. For
Jehovah is my refuge! I, _____, choose
the God Above all gods to shelter me. How then can
evil overtake me, or any plague come near? For he orders his angels to protect me wherever I go. They will
steady me with their hands to keep me from stumbling
against the rocks on the trail. I can safely meet a lion
or step on poisonous snakes, yes, even trample them
beneath my feet! For the Lord says, "Because he loves
me, He will rescue me; He will make me great because

I trusts in His name. When I call on Him, He will answer; he will be with me in trouble, and rescue me and honor me. He will satisfy me with a full life, and give me my salvation."

Amen ! And So It Is!

SPREADING THE BLESSING

Living your life for the Lord causes you to realize how unimportant things of the world are. This is by no means to infer that we should live as a pulpier; poor and tattered with our hand out for help at every turn. The Lord will give to us the desires of our hearts, but He commands that we give to others as he gives to us. When He gives much, we are to give much.

Allow yourself to trust the Holy Ghost. Once you've given yourself to Our Heavenly Father and accepted Christ Jesus as your Lord and Savior, He will direct you through His Holy Spirit which lives within you now that you have been saved. When your heart indicates that you should do something, don't question it, just do it. You can not out give God's kindness, nor can you place yourself in the line of danger when you are following His direction. Your obedience will be rewarded greatly from your Heavenly Father who admires your display of love and obedience.

People who are not spiritually aware refer to this revealing as their first mind talking to them. However, much to my surprise, I became aware that this is how God sometimes communicate His desires to us.

God has given each of us dominion over our own hearts and minds. He has given us the decision as to our plight in life. I feel there is no easy way to live in this world seeing that Adam and Eve destroyed that possibility when they, by disobeying God, introduced sin producing evil into our existing situation. However, it has been my determination to consider what the outcome of my life will offer. Do I want to be remembered as one who cared about no one, and had no interest in living according to the Will of God, or would I prefer to be remembered as one, who against all appearance of odds and worldly desires, grasped the hand of her Creator who showed her the way to the Light of Jesus?

My mentor, a very fine lady who was also in the world at one time, and I laugh when we talk about how much we love the Lord, and about our position before Jesus when He returns. In one of our lengthy telephone conversations. I said,

> "In the last days, when Jesus sitting on His Throne, next to the Father, chooses the righteous ones from the crowds of people that will be standing in front of Him crying out, 'Lord don't you remember me.' He will extend His hand outward and say to the crowds, 'Step aside, let her through.'
> With His hand extended in my direction, He will motion for me to come to the front and He'll say to me, 'You don't have to stand out there on line. You accepted and did the Will of my Father. Come here to the front and have a seat.'"

My mentor responded saying of herself,

> "He'll appoint two of His strongest Angels to hold me up; one on each side with their arms under mine to support me. The Crown of Reward placed on my head will be too heavy for me to support without help."

We share the same delight in feelings because of serving the Lord. We are not saying that we are the only people that will be entitled to this glorious treatment. However, we know what we know, because we know and believe the Word. Once you have excepted Christ into your life and began to study to show yourself approved, long to hear and feel His Spirit. Be aware of the times when you truly feel right or wrong in your heart. When an urge to do right overpowers you, and you obey that urge to do right because it pleases God; that is when you'll know that you have aligned yourself with the commands of your Father in Heaven, and you have been truly SAVED.

> James 1:12
> Happy is the man who doesn't give in and do wrong when he is tempted, for afterwards he will get as his reward the crown of life that God has promised those who love Him.

Praise The Lord!

WHEN YOU'RE DOWN TO NOTHING

GOD IS UP TO SOMETHING

FAITH WITHOUT DOUBT

People in this complicated world have grown up with a certain mind set. We think there are many options in which we can choose to direct our lives. Actually there are only two paths that one can take in life, the path of the righteous one, or the path of evil. When the line between the two are straddled, a great deal of confusion is caused in your lives.

We have become accustomed to depending on things or actions that can be seen. We feel lost if there is not an apparent way out of a pinched situation. We must see these things with our own eyes. These are views of a worldly person. The results of this way of thinking is negative, and leads to possible self destructive symptoms such as, alcoholism, depression, nervous breakdowns, loss of control, and serious illnesses brought on by worrying.

> Matthew 6:25-27
> Jesus said; "I tell you, don't worry about your life, what you will eat or drink; or about your body, what you will wear. Is not life more important than food, and the body more important than clothes. Look at the birds in the air. They don't plant or harvest or store food in barns, but your Heavenly Father feeds them. And you know that your are worth much more than the birds. You can not add any time to your life by worrying about it."

It is very realistic that doubt will enter the mind from time to time, especially in the beginning of your walk with Jesus; when you are new in Christ. Uncertainty was introduced into the world as the first sin by the devil himself as a way to discredit our Creator. This is one reason for the many Biblical Scriptures being listed throughout this book It would behoove you to read each one of them; not skipping over any. They will substantiate the truth being the

Facts Of Life According to the Word. Without knowing what Jehovah God has said He will do, and actually proving by doing, one can go through life completely feeling alone to deal with everything that comes along on his own.

The Truth is...the Word is alive and it produces light into your life. You'll find it in the Holy Bible. God said all of it. Doubt is like hunger. The Word is like food. Food feeds hunger and it goes away until it's time to eat again. The truth is God doesn't lie. What God says He'll do, is what God does. How He says He feels about his children, is truly how He feels. God loves us and want us to depend on Him. Unbending--Unending--Unchanging Faith causes you to be what the Almighty truly requires. It will make you right with God, and will guarantee blessings to you.

Mark 11: 23-26 The Amplified Bible
...."Have faith in God constantly. Truly I tell you, whoever says to this mountain, 'Be lifted up, and thrown into the sea! And does not doubt at all in his heart, but believes that what He says will take place, it will be done for him.' For this reason I am telling you, whatever you ask for in payer, believe, trust, and be confident that it is granted to you, and you will get it. And whenever you stand praying, if you have anything

against anyone, forgive him and let it drop, leave it, let it go, in order that your Father who is in Heaven may also forgive you your own failings and shortcomings and let them drop. But if you do not forgive, neither will your Father in Heaven forgive your failings, and shortcomings."

In order to receive the reward of being in God's camp. It is necessary to read His Word, know without a doubt all His Commands, and plant them firmly into your mind and heart. This is the avenue for you to travel to reach His mightiness--His character--His consistency--His love and His forgiveness.

The Spirit of God Almighty is truly awesome. No man walking can do the things that He does. Not even true believers in Christ Jesus, nor those who confess Jesus and quote scriptures in every other sentence, sometimes referred to as 'Stomped Down Christians,' forgive you as many times as God. You are not expected to be perfect, but you are required to repent by asking your Heavenly Father's forgiveness in prayer.

No one is infallible to doubt, not even I. It does enter my mind from time to time even though the intense research that I have done to compile this book has raised my level of faith tremendously. Unfortunately, despite the fact that when this happens, I would love to be able to say, "I know that it is the spirit of evil trying to rob me of my glory and joy-I recognize it immediately because of what I've read in the Bible, and what it has caused my heart to feel", but that's not the case at all. I have allowed myself to be lured into chaos not realizing in advance this is not a happy situation. It was the spirit of evil. I'm speaking of Satan. His job consist of being a master deceiver. His purpose is to steal as many souls as possible. His reasoning is to prove to God that His beloved Creation of Human Beings are corrupt, non-loyal and unappreciative creatures.

He tunes his focus on your minds, convincing you that you're going forward when you are actually moving in a backwards direction. It's not to his benefit to give in easily, seeing that he's out to move you away from serving the God of Creation. The deeper your existence in the ways of the world, the less attention he pays to you. The closer you grow to God, the sneakier he becomes. He will try anything until he has tried everything.

Matthew4:1-11
Jesus was led by the Spirit into the desert to be tempted by the devil. After fasting forty days, and forty nights, he was hungry. The tempter came to him and said, "If

Facts Of Life According To The Word Volume 1

you are the Son of God, Tell these stones to become Bread."

Jesus answered, "It is written: 'Man does not live on bread alone, but on every word that comes from the mouth of God.'"

Then the devil took him to the Holy City and had him stand on the highest point of the temple.

"If you are the Son of God, " He Said, "Throw your self down, for it is written, "He will command his angels concerning you and they will lift you up in their hands so that you will not strike your foot against a stone."

Jesus answered him, "It is also written: 'Do not put the Lord your God to the test.'"

Again, the devil took him to a very high mountain, and showed him all the kingdoms of the world and their splendor. "All this I will give you, "He said, "If you will bow down and worship me."

Jesus said to him, "Away from me, Satan! for it is written: Worship the Lord your God, and serve him only.'" Then the devil left him, and angels came and attended him.

Notice how Jesus listened to Satan intently quoting Scriptures until He was fed up with Satan trying to coerce Him to depart from God and follow him. He simple said, "Satan be on you way." Keep in mind Satan was out of there at Jesus' command. The key is to realize when Satan is on the scene. He doesn't announce his entrance. There is no banner alerting you of his presence. Be assured that if you are doing the work of God, he will be on your tail like white on rice.

A very simple example would be: if you've had problems with anyone in the past, and because you have now accepted Jesus as your Lord and Savior, Satan will come in just when you are ready to forgive that person and put that element of doubt in your mind.

He says to you, "I wouldn't forgive. Don't you remember what they did? I wouldn't let them get away with that."

Sometimes it is so extremely subtle that it's hardly noticeable. If it weren't for the drastic change in opinion about your previous decision to forgive, you could be completely fooled. You'd wonder how your change of heart came about so abruptly. This can send you right back to first base. That's when you must put on the Armor of God remembering all of His promises to those who accept and obey His Commands.

The Armor of God are the Scriptures from the Bible. Jesus said, "When you stand praying forgive all." Tell that to Satan. Simply say, "Satan it is written: When I stand praying, I am to forgive all those who I hold grudges against, so that my Father in Heaven will forgive my imperfections.

Remember that you were taken back from the devil with the suffering death and resurrection of Our Lord Jesus. He redeemed us and set us free from any evil forces having power over us. The blood that our Lord Jesus Christ shed through the abuse that was done to Him protects us. Satan has a fear of the Blood of Jesus. Even the name of Jesus has great power. Test it for yourself. The next unbearable situation that you find yourself being treated unfairly, call out the name if Jesus. If you are in public, you can do it quietly, under your breath. If you're alone you can do it loudly, letting all of the frustration hang out. There is no rule to the sound level. The only thing that is absolutely required is that you believe that the situation will be changed.

Because of the ascension of Christ Jesus, after being crucified, back to the right side of Our Heavenly Father, Satan lost the war. He did not expect what was to truly happen. Satan assumed that after Jesus was crucified by humans, 'Roman Soldiers', being prompted intensely by the leaders of God's chosen people, 'the Jews', Jesus would have been disbelieved by His followers.

Therefore, the message that Jesus came to give to the world would have been disregarded as being words of a false prophet. However, Satan knows that he has lost, but he's banking on the fact that you don't know who the winner is. So he's continuing to play the game as though he's holding the winning hand.

RECOGNIZING THE SPIRIT OF EVIL &

THE TAKING OVER OF THE FLESH

Evil doesn't produce a peaceful atmosphere. Satan's wish is not for us to experience joy and happiness; he wants chaos and turmoil. He delights in confusion. Broken homes, abusive relationships, shattered spirits, and unruly children are the sort of things that give him a charge.

A common example of this is happening in ones home on a daily basis. One that could involve your children. Your wonderful young ones that have, up to now, been as perfect as children can be. Satan has been known to come in with his tricks and lies in an attempt to deter them. He'll have your young ones' doing things that are totally out of character for them. You'll be wondering, "What's going on"? He could use an acquaintance that your child may have acquired; one who is not the type of friend you would want your child to associate with. He is a great deceiver and he doesn't run out of tricks. You see, Satan also use people to deliver his nasty little messages and to do his dirty work. This is just a brief example of how treacherous Satan is, and it is light weight in nature. To give an example of something that is true and current.

While writing The Facts of Life According To The Word, sitting at my computer which is located approximately eight feet away from my front door, and where my children's bicycles are kept chained to the railing on the porch outside, someone ingeniously cut the bike lock from one of my daughters bicycles and stole it. As much as I would like to be a Saint, it wasn't happening. Many terrible thoughts arose in my mind. The desire that I wish to have within me is to carry the cross, but my initial thought was to demolish this person. For most of the day, I thought of what I would have done had I looked out of the peep hole of my door. I tried to dispel the thoughts of puncturing holes into the thief with my dicing knife. Maybe cutting him up in the same manner as I would do an onion. I know that these are ungodly reactions, and I repent for thinking them. However, my worldly ways of defense were surfacing.

When the notifying knock came at the door, I was
jarred. Writing, and rewriting this chapter which lead me to tell the
truth about Satan; his conniving character, his underhanded wittiness
and how he calculates your vulnerabilities, preying upon them, led him
to lodge this attack. Actually he was being dogged out pretty badly.
Although, hearing the mysterious sounds would normally alarm me;
causing me to turn and look around. I realized what I was doing, and
thought this was another one of Satan's ploys. Yes! It was indeed a
very realistic and unexpected maneuver by him. I heard sounds and
actually thought, it was only my mind amplifying creeks that are heard
when silence is upon the settling of a house. I began to ignore them
because I was alerting the world of how he operates in ones life. He
felt a need to stop me, even if it was only momentarily. When you
are doing something that God has told you to do, the demons come
in to play tricks with your mind. That is the normal thought, and it is
correctly so.

Although it is my determination to finish this book,
and I do not intend to let any evil spirits deter what I have been called

to do, the knock at the door rattled me. My now fatigued body sprang

into an upright position in my computer chair. I rose from the chair

realizing that it was a knock on the door, and not a creek in the floor.

It was the middle daughter of my second set of children.

"Hi Mommy, look what I checked out of the

library." She said excitedly when I opened the door.

"Dee Dee, you scared the crap out of me!" I said,
swinging the door open.

I thought the children would be using their keys to

get back into our house.

"I was just telling people how sneaky Satan is; expos-
ing him to the world. I was so startled, I almost fell out
of the chair at the sound of your knock.
"Oh"! she said with wide bright eyes.

Before she could say anything else, the baby girl

walked in.

"Hi Mommy," She said with a big smile.
"Hi Honey," I replied between sentences.

I was still trying to demonstrate to Dee Dee how

I reacted to her knock on the door. I had the attention of two of my

daughters observing my attempt to shake in the chair; displaying my

reaction. The rate of my heart was still thumping fast from the shock.

The door had partially close behind the baby of my three girl's when it flung open again.

"Hi Mommy, where is Dee Dee's bike?" Missy blurted out.

"What!" I said, "What do you mean where is Dee Dee's bike?"

I rose out of the chair that I had been in for hours working on this book, and had seconds ago been demonstrating how the knock on the door had startled me. Walking over to the front door of our small home to look, my older daughter replied,

"Dee Dee's bike is not here Mommy!" Missy continued with a questioning look on her face.

Every one ran back to the door. I pushed my way though trying to see, while hoping my older daughter was, out of the norm, playing a joke on us. Much too my surprise, it was no joke. The sounds that I thought were the settling of structure floors, or possibly Satan trying to play tricks on my mind, was someone cutting the chain of Dee Dee's bicycle, and removing it from being positioned behind Sandra's bike.

I stood in the doorway with a frown of disappointment on my face as Missy pulled the remainder of the cut bike chain from around the railing that it had been attached too. I looked over at Dee Dee to see extremely wide eyes, and a mouth dropped opened. Not wanting her to burst into tears, I quickly said, "We can buy you another bike Dee Dee. Don't worry about it. It's Satan trying to make you think he's in charge."

Like any other loving parent, I felt a strong desire to console my child. I didn't laugh this matter off. It wasn't funny to me. I know this world is filled with evil people. Once upon a time, I wasn't the one for them to confront. Though I never considered my self evil, I had ways, and means to keep evil from penetrating my family's space. I thank the Holy Spirit for diverting my mind to the sound that I was hearing. In the past I would have walked around my house with a weapon in hand to find what was causing the sound. Had it been someone infiltrating my space, his days would have been concluded justifiably by law. In simpler terms, I would have blown him away on my turf. Sounds cold, doesn't it. That's the reason that God extended his hand out to me. He knew that I wasn't a killer. He showed me another way to beat the enemy.

The rest of the day did not go well at all. Depression that one feels when something like this happens turned into a vengeful experience for me. I wanted to do the due to the guy. How dare him invade my space. I silently fought with feelings of revenge all day. Needless to say, I couldn't write any longer.

Dee Dee handled the loss of her bike like a champ. Being the spiritual leader for my children, I tried to stay calm. It was hard work trying to get my rage under control. I prepared dinner as usual, and sat down to the table to hopefully get through this meal without having to discuss this episode with my girls. I knew that I couldn't be very spiritual in displaying my thoughts. We begin to bless our food.

"God is good, God is great,

Let us thank Him for our food.

By His hands we are fed.

Give us Lord our daily bread.

In Jesus name, Amen!"

I had prepared a Tuna Pasta Salad along with a Garden Salad. For the one hundred and ten degree heat of Phoenix, this was a great meal. We were all excited with our platters of the two assorted salads and Ritz crackers. Everyone was into the meal.

"Mommy, this is good," Missy said as she

munched down on a fork full of her favorite Garden Salad.

"Thanks Sweetie" I said, "I'm glad you like it."

Dee Dee, eating as though she would never see food again said,

"Yeah Mom, you put your foot in it."

As I listened to their complements I thought, "Thank you Lord for helping me to do this." He knew what kind of day I was having.

Sandra, the baby girl as I refer to her, lingering behind as usual said, "Mommy this is great."

"Thank you baby."

I felt as though no one was bothered by the event of the day. We could at least have a wonderfully peaceful dinner. Unfortunately dinner is not a very long period of time. I concentrated on the meal waiting for the true joy of the Lord to come back upon me, so that I could get back to the writing of this book. It had already been a few hours since the discovery of the stolen bicycle. I truly wanted that to be a thing of the past, because I don't like being down in the dumps in spirit.

Every one was filling up. Food was still on the

plates, but this was the time that my family starts to have dinner table conversation. Every one complemented the meal once again as they slowed their pace on eating.

"Mommy we would know Dee Dee bike if we saw it again." Missy said.
"Yeah Missy! How could we miss it. It's green neon. I haven't seen one like it around here. "I responded.

Dee Dee was still eating. I glanced over at her out of my peripheral vision not wanting her to see me sneakily observing her demeanor. I was thanking Jesus that this had not affected her in a totally bad way. She seemed to be taking it into stride as she continued to fill her tiny body up with more food than any of the other children ever eat.

"Who do you think it was Mommy?" Asked Missy.

We live in a beautiful, but over populated neighborhood. The ratio of crime is low, however it does exist. I had previously determined that this entire state was filled with petty thieves. Since I've been in Phoenix, Arizona, I've had my car stolen, Missy's very expensive bike stolen, and now Dee Dee's bike. I've had enough of the stealing stuff.

I stopped eating to look at my oldest daughter and said,

"I have no idea Missy,"

Without blinking an eye, and feeling the rage beginning to rise within me again,

I said, "The Holy Spirit was with me. He kept me on the computer even though I was hearing noises that seemed like the settling of this house. Had I gone over to that door, and seen someone out there tampering with our bikes, he would have belonged to me just like those bikes. He would have become a thing, not a person."

At that point, the fury in me was full fledge giving way to some very vicious feelings. I began vividly describing what I would have done to him.

"If I had looked through that peep hole, I would have gotten my dicing knife, opened the door and treated him like he was a Thanksgiving turkey on my table. That is a fact of life according to the world."

This is why I love my Father God so much. His Holy Spirit stepped in and kept me from doing something that I would have regretted for the rest of my life. My carnal mind, and my flesh could have caused me to take one of God's Human beings out. It would have all been over a bicycle valued at only $160.00

However, no amount of money could be an equal to the value of a

human life.

       I was angry. I don't steal anything from anyone,

and I don't want anyone to steal anything from me. Nevertheless, I

wished some pretty bad things to happen to the rogue. I asked that the

Lord let His wrath come down on him, and anyone else who touch that

bike. Then I became more vicious, I suggested that he ride out in front

of an eighteen wheel truck and get smashed. At that point my children

stopped me.

> "Okay Mommy that's enough. Didn't you say that God
> said pray for those that do things against you and he'll
> handle it. What was that about heaping coals of fire on
> the heads of your enemies, Mom."

> "Yeah, you're right, He said if your enemy is thirsty
> give him drink. If he's hungry give him food. In doing
> this you will be heaping hot coals on his head. Thank
> you Missy, I was getting carried away."

       I was happy she stopped me. This is one of those

judgments that I may never see, but I have faith that the Lord is going

to handle this. If it occurs before I'm finished writing, I'll make sure

the results go into the book. I want to share the outcome with you.

Because of my faith in God's Word, I know he will not let my child be with out a bicycle knowing how much she loves to ride.

To the people who are appalled at what I've just said, you are obviously perfect Christians, living in a Christ like existence. However, in my opinion there are more people who would rather take vengeance into their own hands, so they can see themselves receiving satisfactory results even if it is only temporary. Those are the people that this book is being written for.

We need to practice faith. God does supply all of our needs when we accept Christ, and believe that He won the war. Regardless of what Satan sends his demons out to do to you, know that you are more than a conqueror. It's no shame in the game when you have taught your children well, and they bring it back to you in a time of need. I'm proud to have children that stand firm when I loose my balance. That's what the family, and the body of Christ is about. Reminding each other of the Powerful Word of God.

I learned years ago to bind Satan with the Precious Blood that poured from the whip cuts that Jesus sustained, but it didn't penetrate. I wasn't ready for it. I guess God hadn't given me ears to hear. The bruising that made him lose the appearance of a human, and the piercing that was inflicted upon Him by the Roman Soldiers. The agony that He willingly sustained to free us from the wiles of the world have become clear to me now. I am learning more and becoming stronger everyday. I now take full advantage of standing on the Word, and wearing the Armor of God. However, there are times that I have to regroup; as was illustrated previously.

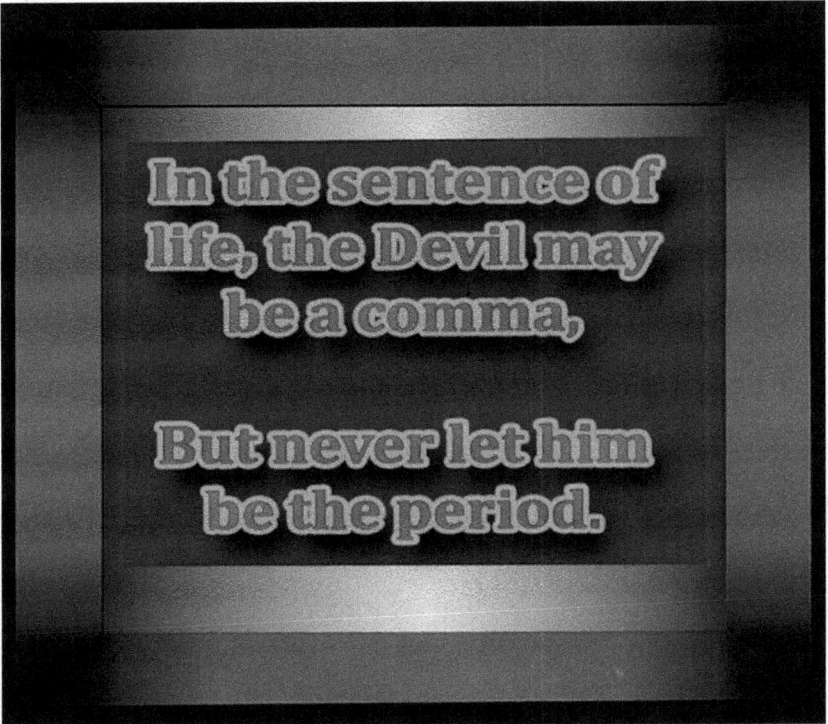

In the sentence of life, the Devil may be a comma,

But never let him be the period.

Do bind Satan. He has no control over you unless you give it to him. Do not refuse to take full advantage, in a positive way, of Jesus' death on the cross, and the power of His Rising. Your defense and protection is to read the Word on a daily basis. Become strong and grow closer every day to Jesus. Associate yourself with people that love Our Father, the Son, and The Holy Spirit. Minister to each other to lift each others spirits. Love each other with the same love that Jesus has for the church, and that God has for His Creation. You'll build an amazing confidence, and will soon come to realize that your faith is growing. This is putting on the Armor of God.

THE BLESSING

This volume of Facts Of Life According To The Word, that you are currently reading, is a revised edition. Because of this, I'm able to give a testimony, as promised. I am revealing the blessing given to our family in rebuttal to the travesty of the stolen bicycle. Although my reaction to the devastating news of the bicycle being stolen, as I was working on the original copy of this book, was extreme anger, we were still blessed.

My family had been existing with only one car. Okay! I know what you're thinking, "Some family's don't have a car at all." Yes! It was a blessing to have a car, but everyone in our house had business outside of our home on a daily basis. My husband had to work. Our oldest daughter was going to a high school located downtown Phoenix. Fortunately our two younger children were attending a school that was within walking distance, but it was my job to walk with them, and meet them after school. We had not quite gotten to the point of allowing them to ride their bikes to school yet. In addition to writing and attending college part time, I had recently gotten a job within walking distance as a Sales Design Specialist which required me to dress in professional attire. This would have been okay except, I had to walk to work in the Phoenix sunny climate. You can see how a second car would have really been helpful.

As with many family's with young children, we do what we have to do. It all comes naturally, without giving it any thought. We also sometimes miss realizing the blessings that we're receiving along the way. As well, I could have missed out on the blessing of receiving an opportunity to take over ownership of a new pickup truck shortly after the theft of the bicycle.

Receiving a call from an acquaintance was a happy day for me. She called to ask if I would take possession of her pick up truck. She had been incapacitated and unable to work. Because of this, she was going to loose her truck for non payments of the monthly notes. Seeing that I had just begun working, and didn't think that I would qualify for a new car purchase, I jumped on it.

"Yes!" I told her. "That would be great."

There was no formality involved. No contracts were signed. The truck would remain in her name. She would maintain the insurance, I would maintain the monthly payments, and take possession of the vehicle. It was a blessing for the entire family. We were now able to do more fun things, not being retrained because of only having one vehicle. It was much more fun for the girls than their bicycles. I let them ride in the back with all their friends whenever we were riding through safe zones. Keep in mind that I'm speaking of Arizona some years ago.   And the story doesn't end there.

A few months later, the owner of the truck called wanting to know if I could loan the truck to her cousin because he was moving. He needed to use it to haul some household items. For the 1st time, I felt accepting this truck may have been a wrong move on my part.

It really had not penetrated my mind and heart of how truly magnificent God is in his workings. It still takes some mind adjustments to keep me from being blown away.

I had to give thought to whether her cousin could use the truck for moving furniture. I did not want to be selfish, but that is exactly what the bottom line was. I also felt she had no right to offer the truck, that I was now paying for, to assist anyone. This was a brand new red truck with no scratches, scuffs, or abrasions on it. It was not the type of vehicle I would have gone to the dealership and said, "I have to have that truck or I'll die," but it was so much fun, and added a little versatility to my lifestyle. It was more like a cute little toy truck you'd pick out as a Christmas gift for a little boy. Only it was in an adult size.

I decided to let her cousin borrow it, after asking her to make sure it was returned without scratches and scrapes from transporting stuff. We made arrangements for the cousin to come to my job to get the keys, and pick up the truck. He was to return it by the time I got off work. Everything went well. He used it, and returned it clean and scar free.

Shortly thereafter, she called to let me know her financial situation had improved, and she would like to have her truck back. Okay! This was not something that I wanted to hear. It was not something that I had expected either, nor was it in the plan as it was presented to me. Needless to say, I tussled with the thought of having to return to a one car family again. I thought of all types of strategies to keep from having to give the truck back. How can I tell someone they can not have something that clearly belongs to them. It was still in her name; she still retained the insurance in her name. The monthly car payments were given to her, so she was the one sending the money to the finance company.

As I fretted, moaning and groaning to my husband; telling him that I will not give it back. I never considered the fact that she needed her means of getting around as well. She had worked for the truck, but ran into hard times. The idea of me taking over the payments of the vehicle was not discussed in a manner declaring she would be taking it back once she was on her feet again. This very important bit of information, that had been left out, was not only her fault. It was my fault as well for not treating it like a business deal, and requiring a contract with all the stipulations to be signed. Obviously that was not the way it was suppose to play out though... I was to learn a lesson from this.

James 4:2
You want what you don't have, so you kill to get it.
You long for what others have, and can't afford it, so
you start a fight to take it away from them. And yet the
reason you don't have what you want is that you don't
ask God for it.

I didn't go to those extremes, but I was thinking
and thinking and trying to come up with some way that I could keep
the truck. Some of my ideas were just downright evil. I'm ashamed
to say that, in a brief moment of fury, I even thought of destroying the
truck. And the story becomes deeper. In Gods' infinite wisdom and
capability, the plan continued.

After a few days of fretting, my husband told
me to give the truck back. I figured, "What the heck. She wanted it
back, and there was nothing that I could do about it considering all
the legalities surrounding it--- but to give it back." So I called her and
made arrangements to return the keys.

Within that week, while supposedly just out driving
around with my husband, we wound up at a Plymouth Dealership.
I had previously seen a Neon, and made mention in passing, that it
was a cute little car. Unbeknown to me, my husband retained that

comment. The next thing I know, I'm test driving a Neon which I liked. Following that, I drove it off the car lot; in my name, with no money down, and 4 months on a job. This was truly unexplainable. There was no way that I should have been able to qualify according normal car purchasing standards, other than God intervened. I was not ready to push my faith to that point, so my husband did it for me.

There are many times that we miss our blessings because of a lack of faith. Actually, this happens more than we can imagine, or more than we would want to admit. This especially applies to us Christians who want to claim that our faith is so strong. The lady owning the truck was a Christian women. That's the reason that I didn't feel as though a contract was important. The offer came so unexpectedly. The timeliness was perfect. I needed a vehicle, and she needed financial help. Our Father in Heaven put us together to help one another. When she no longer needed my help. He placed me in a position to continue with what I needed. He supplied me with my own brand new car. It was a miracle that was taking place in parts. God was still working the plan.

I had become content with only one car in the family. Having a second car was a luxury. We were a happy family.

I'm sure it was because of God. I was working on a project that was assigned to me by Him. Allow me to make this statement mimicking St. Paul,

> "I know what it is to be in need, and I know what it is to have plenty. I have learned the secret of being content in any and every situation, whether well fed or hungry, whether living in plenty or in want." Philippians 4:12.

I always put a special effort forth to not take on a hopeless attitude, or to speak negative words into existence. It's not always easy, but it always pays off to stay positive and to look for God in all situations of your life.

The Neon was great. I had freedom. My own car, with my own insurance allowed me to be able to teach my 15 year old to drive. That was a big help. Now I could give her the keys, and have her run some of my errands for me.

It's a job for both parents to work, and maintain dropping off and picking up children from schools, and activities. There are always turbulences, and schedule malfunctions. I was always the one that would have to give up the job if I couldn't make it work.

So here I was juggling to be the Super Mom.

By our daughters sixteenth birthday, she was ready to take the driving test to get her drivers license. 'Here's the mind blower.' My husband, once again pushing his faith, had me meet him at a dealership to look at a car that he liked. Everything was going along smoothly, so I thought we'd work with what we had. But that was not what he had in mind. We left the car lot that night with two automobiles that were 1 year old. My husband chose a family vehicle. His choice was a Customized Chevy Van. He also chose for me to have a year old Catera Cadillac. Because the Neon was only one year old as well, we would have lost money by trading it in, so we kept it. Once again, we bought these cars with no money down. Our sixteen year old was presented the keys to the Neon for her sixteenth birthday gift. All of this took place within 1 year and 4 months.

The children went from riding bicycles to driving and riding in their own car. Who knew? I was following what God was telling me to do, which was writing the original copy of this book. I can attest that when you realize God has given you something to do.... 'do it'.... and don't stop until it's done.

I heard a minister say that God doesn't take anything away from you, it's Satan. That is not completely true. When God puts you on a course; and you leave that course, whatever blessing you are receiving from being on that course will stay on that course, whether you remain on it or not. Maybe that minister should have been more clear in his deliverance. Maybe God doesn't take it away. You leave it when you leave what God is telling you to do. That's another story that I won't get into right now. Keep following me. I'm giving a 101 class on how faith, while following God, works. It is all coming from Him, but being written down by me.

WHAT IS AN EQUAL YOKE?

2 Corinthians 6:14-18
Do not be teamed with unbelievers. Don't be teamed with those who do not love the Lord, for what do the people of God have in common with the people of sin? How can light live with darkness? And what harmony can there be between Christ, and the devil? How can a Christian be a partner with one who doesn't believe? And what union can there be between God's temple and idols? For you are God's temple, the home of the living

God, and God has said of you, "I will live in them and walk among them, and I will be their God, and they shall be my people." That is why the Lord has said, "Leave them; separate yourselves from them; don't touch their filthy things, and I will welcome you, and be a Father to you, and you will be my sons and daughters.

Christians and Non-Christians, in any aspect, have no chance of success in a relationship. This includes race, nationality, and business. The thought pattern poses obvious conflicts between the two. One who is mature in his Christian beliefs will know that he can rely on the Holy Spirit for direction and protection. The non-Christian will always follow what he is able to see with his eyes. In a business ventures, this frame of mind will obviously present division in thoughts, and ideas. If this can not be overcome, it will inevitably bring on a dissolution of their business partnership.

People of other countries have other customs. Sometimes they worship other gods. There are nationalities that choose to serve the Almighty God, but refuse to accept Jesus Christ as the Son of God. The Creator will not occupy the same space as a statue that has been made by human hands, and called a god. Not accepting Jesus as Lord and Savior denies you the wonderful covering of His Blood. There is a guarantee that even though you were created by the Living God, He will not be listening or responding to you. You are just another lost, unsaved soul out there on your own who will have to answer for the decisions you've made.

The race card is played often in this world; not taking into consideration the fact that Jehovah God created all human beings, and that we are all the same inside and out, except for the coloring of our skin. This has positioned certain ethnic groups in non negotiable situation. There has been a great effort put forth to suppress the black and the brown skinned people of this world. The longevity of this plan has actually caused great confusion, seemingly, in the minds of many as to what is right, and what is wrong.

The fact is, God loves colors. Everything that He spoke into existence has color. The flowers has an array of colors and hues. The trees are varied with shades of green, orange and yellows. The bodies of water; rivers, lakes, oceans and streams are a cascade of white, light blue, dark blue, greens and in the deep sea, the water appears to be dark grey. The coloring of the skies are the most magnificent of all. In areas that have not been totally infused by industry and automobile pollution, the arrangement in colors of purple, orange, red, blue and yellow are absolutely breathtaking. At night the glittering stars sparkle through black layering. It is a most beautiful sight to behold. God designed and created His Human Beings to come in many shades of light and dark tones of brown and white. When seen in a group, this is also a sight to behold.

I have graphically stressed this point to prove the colorfulness of God. How could a group of people be un-teamed with a race of another color. It is not possible based upon the color of ones skin. The problems that exist are created because of cultural prejudices. I'm sure God didn't intend for this to happen. That was not His plan. Sounds like some of Satan's handy work to me. See how well he does his job: He has some of us hating each other based on skin color. We have got to come to the realization of what the real deal is. We can not continue to let our minds be manipulated.

To worship the Lord intently with excitement; and to be yoked to someone, in any aspect of your life, who does the same is the requirement of Jehovah God. It will keep you on the righteous path, and under the protection of the Holy Spirit. This happens because everyone involved knows that all things are possible when God is the headliner of the show.

O MIGHTY GOD

"Let the Power of the Holy Spirit come upon the readers of these words, Send your Mighty Angels to surround them in their circumstances. Keep their families safe from any unrighteous forces that are trying to pursue them. Give them ears to hear, eyes to see, and a discerning heart to know your Spirit.

In Jesus Name, I Pray Amen!

Wisdom is given to me by the Power of the Holy Spirit. God's Angels protect me as they bring my many blessings, and it's wonderful to know that they're there. This is the power of Faith Without Doubt. It is such a feeling of relief to know that no trauma can over come me. I have faith that God has a plan for my life. It will include trials and tribulations which God has engineered. He uses hard times to build our strength, help us to deal with our weaknesses and test our faith, He will measure our progress by our capacity to endure.

THE BENEFITS OF WALKING THE WALK

James 1:2-8
Consider it pure joy, my brothers, whenever you face trials of many kinds because you know that the testing

of your faith develops perseverance. Perseverance must finish its work so that you may be mature and complete not lacking anything. If any of you lacks wisdom, he should ask God, who gives generously to all without finding fault, and it will be given to him. But when he asks, he must believe and not doubt, because he who doubts is like a wave of the sea, blown and tossed by the wind. That man should not think he will receive anything from the Lord; he is a double-minded man, unstable in all he does.

James 1:12-13
Blessed is the man who perseveres under trial, because when he has stood the test, he will receive the crown of life that God has promised to those who love him. When tempted, no one should say, "God is tempting me." For God cannot be tempted by evil, nor does he tempt anyone; but each one is tempted when, by his own evil desire, he is dragged away and enticed. Then after desire has conceived, it gives birth to sin; and sin, when it is full grown, gives birth to death.

The benefits of living in the Will of God are such that one, who functions according to the ways of the world, can not imagine. "This must be the end of life," would be the initial thought of a person who is unaware of a more perfect alternative. How can a person possibly have more fun thinking, talking about, and praising God, not to mention associating with other people that think the same way? It sounds boring, and dry to someone who has never experienced delighting themselves with the Power of God. This will offer an incentive that will stimulate your mind and give you food for thought.

> Psalm 112:6-8
> The uncompromisingly righteous, the upright, in right standing with God shall be in everlasting remembrance. He shall not be afraid of evil tidings; His heart is firmly fixed, trusting leaning on and being confident in the Lord. His heart is established and steady, he will not be afraid while he waits to see his desire established upon his adversaries.

> Psalm 119:1-3
> Happy are all who perfectly follow the laws of God. Happy are all who search for God, and always do his Will, rejecting compromise with evil, and walking only in His paths.

Living a pure life is my earnest desire. Because I've given myself to My Father in Heaven, He is helping me by extending patience and tenderness, while molding me into an example of the Christ nature, and putting me on the right path. This is the path that I once believed I was on. Much to my surprise I was border-lining the world. I had to allow myself to be deprogrammed. It was necessary to adjust my own priorities putting my Heavenly Father first.

> Matthew 6:33-34
> But seek; aim for, and strive after, first of all, His kingdom and His righteousness, His way of doing and being right and then all these things, taken together will be given to you besides. So don't worry or be anxious about tomorrow, for tomorrow will have worries and anxieties of its own. Sufficient for each day is its own trouble

MONEY, MONEY, MONEY, MO---NEY

Money being the almighty priority in many peoples lives has had a major impact on their choices. It once was a major factor in my life. I never thought I would love anything more than money, except my children. I realized that those priorities had to be readjusted.

On a beautifully clear morning, while driving

downtown on I285 in Atlanta, Georgia, I tuned the radio onto one of the secular stations only to hear them playing a particular song whose chorus lines rang out melodiously: "Silver and Gold! Silver and Gold! I'd rather have Jesus, than Silver and Gold. "Although my attention was deep seated in the lyrics, and floating with the smooth sound of voices delivering the rhythm, I found myself saying,

"I love you Jesus, but I love gold too."

I was really out there, as are many others, when it comes to making a decision between money, and God.

t can gold do for anyone if they have some incurable illness? What can it do if their hearts are broken, and their spirit have sunk to an all time low; Until their minds are in a state of depression that can't be shaken? What can gold do to insure that ones' children truly love, honor, and respect them? No amount of gold can buy true love. However, it can make some dramatize an act, pretending to love you. Gold is not everything. On this point people who make their living relying solely on themselves, and their gold, would argue me down.

I know the feeling of losing the love of a child and wondering how this could have happened. The love that I extended was greater than life itself. As a matter of fact, two of my children

163

who are now adults seem to have a nonchalant attitude towards me. One child does show her hostility much more than the other. Her display of feelings diminished, despite the fact that I gave material things, that gold buys as well as myself, to her. I felt, and continue to feel I was always there for her. If gold could bring them back, the relationships wouldn't be real. My daughter would have never left. She was there to reap the benefits of all my illegal, as well as legal activities. Only the Good Lord can rectify the relationship, and I have faith without doubt that He will in time, now that I've put my priorities in order. I say now, because as I am writing this book, I am getting answers to questions that I've had. For instance, "Why would a child shown much love, turn extremely cold towards a parent without some logical reason?" The Spirit within me has reminded me of my past priorities; "How can I expect more than I have given?" From deep within my heart a declaring came forth, "You didn't give love to your Father in Heaven nearly like you did your children, especially the child who so drastically turned against you. As a matter of fact, you allowed your Creator Father to rank pretty low on that priority list of yours."

My Father Yahweh gives, He has the power to do so. He can take away as well; this is also within His Power. I've said it before, and I'll say it again, and again until the point that, 'Without God nothing is forever,' penetrates your brain waves.

I have been cared for by Jehovah Jireh; my Provider. He has provided me ways and means only befitting a King's Kid, even though I didn't deserve it. He rescued me when I couldn't help myself. He answered my little shallow prayers with great blessings; My whimsical desires, He accommodated in abundance. His Grace embraced me as He allowed time for me to come around. I realized that it was, in fact, He who had taken full charge of my life. He waited patiently while I rode the roller coaster of life; Up and down, down and up. While I placed blame on anyone for my not being able to stay on top in the money game. I took His love for granted, mainly because I didn't realize that His love was really real.

Coming down from the financial high that I was on was quite a boom. I don't know if my Heavenly Father orchestrated the plop onto the bottom because of all the unfulfilled promises that I made to Him; if only He would let my endeavors be successful, or if He was just trying to get my attention. I prefer to think of it as a learning experience now that I know, and communicate with Him. The fact is, I went through three long years of moaning over the depletion of my money, my business, and all of my worldly possessions.

It was a sad time in my life. I felt it was over forever. I never considered the point that I had been blessed with five wonderfully healthy children, or that the only times that I had ever required hospitalization had been to have my tonsils removed and to give birth to my children. This in itself is a miracle. The fact that I wake up every morning able to thank the Lord for another day, and knowing that He will supply all my needs in that day, is glorious. As for an abundance of money, I have not ruled that out. I'm standing on Gods' Word that He will give me the desires of my heart. This time I will allow Him to direct what I should do with it.

THE EVIL FORCES OF THIS WORLD

Unfortunately, many people are subjecting themselves, unknowingly, to being ruled by evil forces. The fact that more people are fighting against their Creator than those walking with Him is not an indication that evil has won any war. You can command Satan to go under your feet and be trampled in the Name of Our Lord Christ Jesus. Stifle his movement in your lives by putting on the armor that prevents any evil penetration. Satan can't change the course of the wind, nor can he prevent the sun from rising on the new day, and he certainly can not stop a blessing that your Heavenly Father wants to give to you, if you do not allow him too. What he can do, is fool you by lying to you, and playing games with your mind which will cause you to permit a fiasco to come into your situation. He can make an occurrence seem so terribly hopeless until you worry to the point of making your body extremely ill' or worry yourself to death, 'Yes', to death. Do you know what he does then? He dances around with the group of outcast angels, who have now become 'homies' of the evil one, and celebrate. 'Another one bites the dust'. He lives to tempt Gods children, just as he tried to tempt Jesus.

First of all, please let me point out to you readers. 'saints and non-saints,' Satan chooses your weakest moment in which to strike. You are prime meat to give in if you are not standing on the Word of God. Secondly, nether this world, nor anything in it belongs to Satan, so how can he give it to you. As we know, the very Pit of Hell (Hades) belongs to Satan. Hell belongs to his demons and all those that have chosen to continued to sin without reservation, and have refused salvation form Christ Jesus. God created it that way, and designated it as home for the Evil One, and his Partners. As my Mom would say, "Misery loves company." Satan has to be miserable knowing that his final destination is the Pit, located in the core of this earth, to be chained for a very long time. Why not entice you to join him. After all, company would be great. So he gets you to join him by convincing you, or making a deal with you to do things that you know are wrong.

> He says, "You shouldn't love your neighbor, as you love yourself."
> He convinces you, "Do not honor your Creator with your body, mind and heart." He wants you to believe that you just appeared on this earth one day. Or maybe you evolved from an Ape. However, you don't have to be thankful to anyone.
> He's saying, "Shoot your neighbor and take what belongs to him. Go forcefully in the middle of the night and delete the entire family. You'll have the money to buy the Crack-Cocaine that will send your mind to the moon for three minutes."
> He's saying to the men, "Go have sex with as many women as you can; let your semen enter their canals, and join with the eggs that will produce more wonderful lives for us to steal. You won't have to worry about caring for and loving these children. The more the merrier.
> Women, don't be concerned with being promiscuous."
> He persuasively suggest, "Let your desires run rampant. Don't ask the name of your bed partners for

the night. After all, you don't want to marry them, you only want to sex them. When you're satisfied, just say to them; 'don't call me, I'll call you.'"

Satan is convincing the world that not only is it okay to change your sex, it's also okay to marry someone who is the same sex. It's okay to have annual parades to exhibit the defiance of the Word of God. It's okay to teach this vile behavior in public schools that all tax payers must contribute too.

He speaks to our young people misusing the fact that their minds are underdeveloped, and innocent. This allows many of them to be easily convince;

"You don't have to love and honor your mother and father. They just want to tell you what to do, always ragging on you about going to church and to school. Trying to help you choose, what they term, good, positive friends to associate with. What do parents know"? Your parent don't know what's happening. They're living in another world, in another time. They can't relate to getting bombed out of their minds and terrorizing people. They don't know that this Crystal Meth that I have for you will transform you into a bird, and you'll be able to fly off a 50 story building."

He tirelessly convinces people of all ages, "You don't have to love anyone, not even yourself."

Satan is the one and only who has some of the so called 'Men of God' (ministers, preachers, reverends, pastors) out there in man ordained churches giving Christianity a very bad name. They have been self consecrated by their own word, and are now distorting Gods' Word. They cause many to not want to follow the Creators Rules.

WAKE UP!

Do you think Our Heavenly Father can not put a stop this? God can do this, but you have been given a choice. There is a predestination for your life. There is a purpose in this life time, in this world for you. Unless you are fulfilling the intended plan for your life, you will always lack something. Also you will have left the door wide open for the evil one to enter. You may have all the money you need or want, but you won't have happiness and joy. I'm sure I don't have to tell you how absolutely uncomfortable the lack of peace of mind is.

You're probably thinking that I am being very presumptuous in assuming that everyone who does not follow the Order of God will have major problems. If not yet, sooner or later. I can personally guarantee you that there will be some void. Something that comes into your life when you're all alone; late at night, or early in the morning. It can strike at any time. You don't recognize it at first. You think you have everything. 'What can the matter be?' The matter is, you are relying on yourself.

The original intent for Gods' Creation was not to live apart from His Divine Direction. You can not direct yourself. You are to go to God in prayer with everything that you wish to do, as you wish to do it. This will prevent you from running into blockades. You need the power that the Blood of Jesus has afforded you to move mountains, and call into existence any good thing that your heart desires. A true, active relationship with Almighty God, and Faith that His Word is true, will cause Miracles to come forth in your life.

Doubt is a negative; a terrible thing to allow in a time when a right decision must be made, especially when you believe in the Lords Word. What you are subconsciously saying is, "I don't really believe God can do anything, I'm just saying that he can." You have instantly blocked any blessings that you would have received.

Jesus doesn't need doubting followers. He is the Son of God, and in very high-ranking position. He has earned His position to be at the right hand side of The Heavenly Father. He established his throne for judgment when He allowed Himself to be a sacrifice as an atonement for our sins. We need to be saying, "Thank

You Jesus!"

> Psalms 9:7-9
>
> All who are oppressed may come to Him. He is a refuge for them in their times of trouble. All those who know your mercy Lord, will count on you for help, for you have never yet forsaken those who trust in you.

> Psalm 37:4-5
>
> Be delighted with the Lord. Then he will give you all your heart's desires. Commit everything you do to the Lord. Trust him to help you do it, and he will.

STANDING FIRM based on Daniel 3:1-30

FOUR MEN IN A FIERY FURNACE

This is a story of extreme faith. Every time it's read by me, my faith is refreshed and increased. It depicts a seemingly no win situation in which God intervened and rescued His Children. Although, one may think this only occurred during Biblical times, I assure you that His power, and concerns has not diminished in these days.

> King Nebuchadnezzar made a gold statue ninety feet high, and nine feet wide, and set it up on the Plain of Dura in the province of Babylon; he sent messages to all the princes, governors, captains, judges, treasurers, counselors, sheriffs, and rulers of all the provinces

of his empire to come to the dedication of his statue.
When they had all arrived and were standing before
the monument, a herald shouted out, "O people of all
nations and languages, this is the King's command;
"When the band strikes, you are to fall flat on the
ground to worship King Nebuchadnezzar's gold statue,
anyone who refuses to obey will immediately be thrown
into a flaming furnace.'" So when the band began to
play, everyone--whatever his nation, language, or reli-
gion--fell to the ground and worshiped the statue. But
some officials went to the king and accused some of the
Jews of refusing to worship!
"Your Majesty," they said to him, "you made a law
that everyone must fall down and worship the gold
statue when the band begins to play, and that anyone
who refuses will be thrown into a flaming furnace. But
there are some Jews out there--Shadrach, Meshach, and
Abednego, whom you have put in charge of Babylonian
affairs--who have defied you, refusing to serve your
gods or to worship the gold statue you set up."
Then Nebuchadnezzar, in a terrible rage, ordered
Shadrach, Meshach, and Abednego to be brought in before him. "Is it true, O Shadrach, Meshach, and Abednego," he demanded, "that you are refusing to serve my
gods or to worship the gold statue I set up? I'll give
you one more chance. When the music plays, if you
fall down and worship the statue, all will be well. But
if you refuse, you will be thrown into a flaming furnace
within the hour. And what God can deliver you out of

my hands then?"

Shadrach, Meshach, and Abednego replied, "O Nebu-chadnezzar, we are not worried about what will happen to us. If we are thrown into the flaming furnace, our God is able to deliver us; and he will deliver us out of your hand, Your Majesty. But if He doesn't, please understand, Sir, that even then, we will never under any circumstance, serve your gods, or worship the gold statue you have erected."

Then Nebuchadnezzar was filled with fury and his face became dark with anger at Shadrach, Meshach, and Abednego. He commanded that the furnace be heated up seven times hotter than usual, and called for some of the strongest men of his army to bind Shadrach, Me-shach and Abednego, and throw them into the fire. So they bound them tight with ropes, and threw them into the furnace fully clothed. And because the King, in his anger had demanded such a hot fire in the furnace, the flames leaped out and killed the soldiers as they threw them in! So Shadrach, Meshach, and Abednego fell down bound into the roaring flames.

But suddenly, as he was watching, Nebuchadnezzar jumped up in amazement and exclaimed to his advisors, "Didn't we throw three men into the furnace?" "Yes," they said, "we did indeed, Your Majesty."

"Well, look?" Nebuchadnezzar shouted, "I see four men, unbound, walking around in the fire, and they aren't even hurt by the flames! And the fourth looks like a God!

Then Nebuchadnezzar came as close as he could to the open door of the flaming furnace and yelled: "Shadrach, Meshach, and Abednego, servants of the Most High God! Come out! Come here!" So they stepped out of the fire.

Then the princes, governors, captains, and counselors crowded around them, and saw that the fire hadn't touched them--not a hair of their heads was singed; their coats were un-scorched, and they didn't even smell of smoke!

Nebuchadnezzar said, "Blessed be the God of Shadrach, Meshach, and Abednego for he sent his angel to deliver his trusting servants when they defied the King's commandment, and were willing to die rather than serve or worship any God except their own. Therefore, I make this decree, that any person of any nation, language, or religion, who speaks a word against the God of Shadrach, Meshach and Abednego shall be torn limb from limb, and his house knocked into a heap of rubble. for no other god can do what this one does." Then the king gave promotions to Shadrach, Meshach and Abednego, so that they prospered greatly there in the province of Babylon.

This has always been inspiring reading for me. It reminds me of how powerful God is. It gives my faith a terrific boost during times when it is desperately needed. However, I always assumed that God delivered Shadrach, Meshach, and Abednego because they honored Him greatly. In fact, they did, but there were very important factors left out of the King James Version of this event.

While researching the period between the Old Testament and The New Testament, I discovered a book of Sacred Writings called The Apocrypha. While looking through the contents of this book, I discovered a chapter called The Song of The Three Holy Children. Much to my surprise, this is what took place inside of the furnace. This portion of the story from the book of Daniel, which is Hebrew Scripture, had erroneously been left out of the King James Version of the Bible.

The three Hebrew men, depicted in the story were Ananias, Azarias and Misael. Their names had been changed by King Nebuchadnezzar when taken into captivity, to Shadrach, Meshach, and Abednego. They were standing on the Word of God. They had put on the Armor of God. Even as they surely faced death, their faith kept them loyal to God; and alive. However, if the fiery furnace had consumed them, their reward would have been even greater.

A DEMONSTRATION OF PRAYER

THE SONG OF THE THREE HOLY CHILDREN

And they walked in the midst of the fire, praising God and blessing the Lord. Then Azarias stood up, and prayed in this manner; and opening his mouth in the midst of the fire said:

"Blessed art thou, O Lord God of our fathers thy name is worthy to be praised, and glorified for evermore: For thou art righteous in all the things that thou has done to us. Yea, true are all thy works. Thy ways are right, and all thy judgments truth. In all the things that thou has brought upon us, and upon the Holy City of our fathers, even Jerusalem, thou has executed true judgment:

 For according to truth and judgment did thou bring all these things upon us because of our sins. For we have sinned and committed iniquity, departing from thee. In all things have we trespassed, and not obeyed thy commandments, nor kept them, neither done as thou has command us, that it might go well with us.

Wherefore, all that thou has brought upon us, and everything that thou has done to us, thou has done in true judgment. And thou did deliver us into the hands of lawless enemies, most hateful forsakes of God, and to an unjust king, and the most wicked in all the world.

And now we cannot open our mouths, we are become a shame and disgrace to thy servants, and to them that worship thee. Yet deliver us not up wholly, for thy name's sake, neither remove thy covenant; And cause not thy mercy to depart from us, for thy beloved Abraham's sake, for thy servant Isaac's sake, and for thy Holy Israel's sake; To whom, thou has spoken and promised that thou would multiply their seed as the stars of heaven, and as the sand that lie upon the seashore.

For we, O Lord are become less than any nation, and be kept under this day in all the world because of our sins. Neither is there at this time prince, or prophet, or leader, or burnt offering, or sacrifice, or oblation, or incense, or place to sacrifice before them and to find mercy.

Nevertheless, in contrite heart and an humble spirit let us be accepted. Like as in the burnt offerings of rams and bullocks, and like as in the thousands of fat lambs; So let our sacrifice be in thy sight this day, and that we may wholly go after thee: for they shall not be confounded that put their trust in thee.

And now, we follow thee with all our heart, we fear thee and seek thy face. Put us not to shame; but deal with us after thy loving-kindness, and according to the not to shame: but deal with us after they loving-kindness, and according to the multitude of they mercies. Deliver us also according to thy marvelous works, and give glory to thy name, O Lord; and let all them that do thy servants hurt, be ashamed'; And let them be confounded in all their power and might, and let their strength be broken; and them know that thou are Lord, the only God, and glorious over the whole world."

The King's servants, that put them in, ceased not to make the oven hot with rosin, pitch, tow and small wood, so that the flame streamed forth above the furnace forty and nine cubit. And passed through, and burned those Chaldeans it found about the furnace.

But the angel of the Lord came down into the oven together with Azarias and his fellows, and smote the flame of the fire out of the oven' And made the midst of the furnace as it had been a moist whistling wind, so that the fire touched them not at all. Neither hurt nor troubled them. Then the three, as out of one mouth, praised, glorified, and blessed God in the furnace saying:

Blessed are thou, O Lord God of our fathers:

and to be praised and exalted above all for ever.

And blessed is thy glorious and holy name:

and to be praised and exalted above all for ever.

Blessed are thou in the temple of thine holy glory:

and to be praised and glorified above all forever.

Blessed art thou that beholds the depths, and sit upon the cherubim;

and to be praised and exalted above all for ever.

Blessed art thou on the glorious throne of thy kingdom:

and to be praised and glorified above all for ever.

O all ye works of the Lord, bless ye the Lord;

praise and exalt him above all for ever.

O ye Heavens, bless ye the Lord'

praise and exalt him above all for ever.

O ye Angels of the Lord, bless ye the Lord;

praise and exalt him above all for ever.

O all ye waters that be above the Heaven,

bless ye the Lord; praise and exalt him above all for ever.

O ye powers of the Lord, bless ye the Lord;

praise and exalt him above all forever.

O ye sun and moon, bless ye the Lord

praise and exalt him above all forever.

O every shower and dew, bless ye the Lord;

praise and exalt him above all for ever.

O all ye winds, bless ye the Lord;

praise and exalt him above all for ever.

O all ye fire and heat, bless ye the Lord;

praise and exalt him above all for ever.

O ye winter and summer, bless ye the Lord;

praise and exalt him above all for ever.

O ye dews and storms of snow, bless ye the Lord;

praise and exalt him above all for ever.

O ye nights and days, bless ye the Lord;

praise and exalt him above all for ever.

O ye light and darkness, bless ye the Lord;

praise and exalt him above all for ever.

O ye ice and cold, bless ye the Lord;

praise and exalt him above all for ever.

O ye ice and cold, bless ye the Lord;

praise and exalt him above all for ever.

O ye frost and snow, bless ye the Lord;

praise and exalt him above all for ever.

O ye lightning and clouds, bless ye the Lord;

praise and exalt him above all for ever.

O let the earth bless the Lord;

praise and exalt him above all for ever.

O ye mountains and little hills, bless ye the Lord;

praise and exalt him above all for ever.

O all ye things that grow on the earth, bless ye the Lord;

praise and exalt him above all for ever.

O ye fountains, bless ye the Lord;

praise and exalt him above all for ever.

O ye seas and rivers, bless ye the Lord;

praise and exalt him above all for ever.

O ye whales, and all that move in the waters,

bless ye the Lord; praise and exalt him above all for ever.

O all ye fowls of the air, bless ye the Lord;

praise and exalt him above all for ever.

O all ye beasts and cattle, bless ye the Lord;

praise and exalt him above all for ever.

O Israel, bless ye the Lord;

praise and exalt him above all for ever,.

O ye priests of the Lord; bless ye the Lord;

praise and exalt him above all for ever.

O ye servants of the Lord, bless ye the Lord'

praise and exalt him above all for ever.

O ye spirits and souls of the righteous, bless ye the Lord'

praise and exalt him above all for ever.

O ye holy and humble men of heart, bless ye the Lord;

praise and exalt him above all for ever.

O Ananias, Azarias, and Misael, bless ye the Lord'

praise and exalt him above all for ever;

For he hath delivered us from

hell, and saved us from the hand of death,

and delivered us out of the midst of the furnace and burning flame;

even out of the midst of the fire hath he delivered us.

O give thanks unto the Lord, because he is gracious for his mercy

endures for ever.

O all ye that worship the Lord, bless the God of gods,

praise him, and give him thanks; for his mercy endures for ever.

This true story should have a tremendous impact on one's thought patterns. You should not have to be reminded of how important communicating with God, through prayer, praising and worshipping with song, dance, and raised hands out stretched to Him can be. It has truly won many battles, and stopped many an enemy from executing many acts of harm. It has also caused many a way to be made clear, when there was no way in sight. I know first hand that it brought me back to life after the last breath had left my body lifeless. God relates and responds to our faithfulness and belief. He hears us, and will deliver us out of our bondage.

Instead of worrying over your next crisis, put the Word of God to the test. In sincere honesty and respectfulness, remind Him; "Father God, you said in your word: 'If I delight myself in you, you will give me the desires of my heart." Father my desires are, "(Be specific). Remember, Let our Father know that you are asking through our Lord Jesus Christ. If it were not for what He did for you, you could not do this. Believe that you will receive what you are asking for. Do not become impatient; do not doubt. He will hear you and give anything that is good, to you.

GREAT HEROICS OF FAITH

Hebrews 11:1-40

What is faith? It is the confident assurance that something we want is going to happen. It is the certainty that what we hope for is waiting for us, even though we cannot see it up ahead. Men of God in days of old were famous for their faith.

By faith--by believing god-- we know that the world and the stars-in fact, all things--were made at God's command; and that they were all made from things that can't be seen.

It was by faith that Abel obeyed God and brought an offering that pleased God more than Cain's offering did. God accepted Abel and proved it by accepting his gift; Abel is long dead, but we can still learn lessons from him about trusting God.

Enoch trusted God too, and that is why God took him away to heaven without dying; suddenly he was gone because God took him. Before this happened God had said how pleased he was with Enoch.

You can never please God without faith, without depending on him. Anyone who wants to come to God must believe that there is a God and that he rewards those who sincerely look for him.

Noah was another who trusted God. When he heard God's warning about the future, Noah believed him even though there was then no sign of a flood, and wasting not time, he build the ark and saved his family. Noah's belief in God was in direct contrast to the sin and disbelief of the rest of the world--which refused to obey--and because of his faith he became one of those whom God has accepted.

Abraham trusted God, and when God told him to leave home and go far away to another land which he promised to give him, Abraham obeyed. Away he went, not even knowing where he was going. and even when he reached God's promised land, he lived in tents like a mere visitor, as did Isaac and Jacob, to whom God gave the same promise. Abraham did this because he was confidently waiting for God to bring him to that strong heavenly city whose designer and builder is God.

Sarah, too, had faith, and because of this she was able to become a mother in spite of her old age, for she realized that God, who gave her his promise, would certainly do what he said.

And so a whole nation came from Abraham, who was to old to have even one child--a nation with so many millions of people that, like the stars of the sky and the sand on the ocean shores, there is no way to count them. These men of faith I have mentioned, died with out ever receiving all that God had promised them; but they saw it all awaiting them on ahead and were glad for

they agreed that this earth was not their real home, but
that they were just strangers visiting down here. And
quite obviously when they talked like that, they were
looking forward to their real home in heaven. If they
had wanted to, they could have gone back to the good
things of this world. But they didn't want to. They
were living for heaven. And now God is not ashamed
to be called their God, for he has made a heavenly city
for them.

While god was testing him, Abraham still trusted
in God and his promises, and so he offered up his
son Isaac, and was ready to slay him on the altar of
sacrifice; Yes, to slay even Isaac, through whom God
had promised to give Abraham a whole nation of
descendants: He believed that if Isaac died, God would
bring him back to life again and that is just about what
happened for as far as Abraham was concerned, Isaac
was doomed to death, but he came back again, alive!
It was by faith that Isaac knew God would give future
blessings to his two sons, Jacob and Esau. By faith
Jacob, when he was old and dying, blessed each of
Joseph's two sons as he stood and prayed, leaning on
the top of his cane.

And it was by faith that Joseph as he neared the end of
his life, confidently spoke of God bringing the people
of Israel out of Egypt; and he was so sure of it that he
made them promise to carry his bones with them when
they left!

Moses parents had faith too. When they saw that God

had given them an unusual child, they trusted that God
would save him from the death the king commanded,
and they hid him for three months, and were not afraid.
It was by faith that Moses, when he grew up, refused
to be treated as the grandson of the king, but chose
to share ill-treatment with God's people instead of
enjoying fleeting pleasures of sin. He thought that it
was better to suffer for the promised Christ, than to own
all the treasures of Egypt for he was looking forward to
the great reward that God would give him. And it was
because he trusted God that he left the land of Egypt
and wasn't afraid of the King's anger. Moses kept
right on going; it seemed as though he could see God
right there with him. It was because he believed God
would save his people that he commanded them to kill
a lamb, as God had told them to, and sprinkle the blood
on the doorposts of their homes, as he did among the
Egyptians.

The people of Israel trusted God and went right through
the Red Sea as though they were on dry ground. But
when the Egyptians chasing them tried it, they all were
drowned.

It was faith that brought the walls of Jericho tumbling
down after the people of Israel had walked around them
seven days, as God had commanded them. By faith-
-because she believed in God and his power--Rahab,
the harlot, did not die with all the others in her city
when they refused to obey God, for she gave a friendly
welcome to the spies.

Well, how much more do I need to say? It would take too long to recount the stories of the faith of Gideon, and Barak, and Samson, and Jepthah, and David, and Samuel, and all the other prophets. These people all trusted God and as a result won battles, overthrew kingdoms, ruled their people well, and received what God had promised them. They were kept from harm in a den of lions, and in a fiery furnace. Some, through their faith, escaped death by the sword. Some were made strong again after they had been weak or sick. Others were given great power in battle; they made whole armies turn and run away. And some women, through faith, received their loved ones back again from death. But others trusted God and were beaten to death, preferring to die rather than turn from God and be free--trusting that they would rise to a better life afterwards.

Some were laughed at, their backs cut open with whips; and others were chained in dungeons. Some died by stoning, and some by being sawed in two; others were promised freedom if they would renounce their faith, then were killed with the sword. Some went about in skins of sheep and goats, wandering over deserts and mountains, hiding in dens and caves. They were hungry and sick and ill- treated; too good for this world. And these men of faith though they trusted God and won His approval, none of them received all that God had promised them; for God wanted them to wait and share the even better rewards that were prepared for us.

2 Corinthians 4:16-18

That is why we never give up. Though our bodies
are dying, our inner strength in the Lord is growing
everyday. These troubles and sufferings of ours are,
after all, quite small and won't last very long. Yet
this short time of distress will result in God's richest
blessing upon us forever and ever!
So we do not look at what we can see right now, the
troubles all around us, but we look forward to the joys
in heaven which we have not yet seen. The troubles
will soon be over, but the joys to come will last forever.

Keep the Faith Without Doubt, in all that you do,
and receive your reward from Our Father God...

Hallelujah

WE DON'T CHANGE
GOD'S MESSAGE,

HIS MESSAGE

CHANGES US !

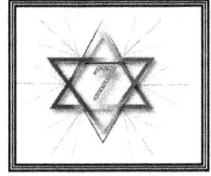

BIBLE CONCORDANCE

Possibly, the difficulty in comprehending the Bible is the terminology used. So many of the words and phrases used are so foreign to the inexperienced Bible readers ears and mind. I prefer to understand what I'm reading. I find great displeasure in reading ten sentences consistently without having a clear picture of what I've just read. Because of the importance of the message that I am wishing to convey, and how the knowledge of it can change your perception, I included this section of a short list of words that are common in the Bible, and what they actually mean in the biblical sense. This will definitely help the reader to relate to the wording of the Bible and to bring the message from Scriptural verses into your hear

Abraham - The father of the Jewish nation. God called Abraham out of his home country and promised to give him the land of Canaan. God also promised that all the people on earth would be blessed through Abraham

Adam - The first man God created. He did not obey God and brought sin and death into the world. Jesus is compared to Adam because Jesus is a new beginning for the human race. Jesus brings new life to those who believe in him.

Adultery - Breaking the marriage promise by having sexual relations with someone other than your husband or wife.

Alien - A person from another country; a stranger.

Altar - A place where people would bring gifts to God. Altars were usually flat on top. They were made of dirt, rocks, wood, or metal.

Amen - 'Yes, this is true!' 'Let it be so' or 'And So It Is.'

Anoint - To pour oil on a person's head, it meant that Gods Spirit was helping that person do a special job.

Antichrist - Means 'against Christ.' In the last days a great evil power called the Antichrist will rule.

Apostles - The special leaders Jesus chose to bring the message about Jesus to the world. First, Jesus chose 12 men, and then later Paul and some others became apostles. Ark of the Covenant - A special box made of wood and covered with gild. It had two gold angels on top of it. The written copy of the Ten Commandments was kept inside the box. The box. The Ark of the Covenant was a sign to the people of Israel that God was with them.

Atonement - A payment or offering to remove or forgive sins. In the Old Testament, the people of Israel sacrificed animals to show that atonement must be made for the sins of the people. When Jesus came, he gave up his own life to make atonement for the sins of his people.

Baal - The name of a false god that means 'master'. The people of Canaan believed Baal had power over the land, crops, and animals.

Babylon - The capital city of Babylonia. The Babylonians captured and destroyed Jerusalem and took many people as prisoners. Later in the Bible Babylon becomes a symbol for evil forces that are against God.

Baptize - to wash, dip or immerse in water. Baptism shows that a person's sins are washed away. He or she has joined the family of God and is united with Jesus in dying to sin and rising to new life.

Bless, Blessing - When God blesses someone, he makes things go well for him or her. A blessing is a good gift from God. When people bless, they ask God to bring good to someone.

Blood - in the Bible, blood represents the life of something. It was the blood of a sacrifice that made it effective.

Canaan - the land God promised to give to Israel. Canaan is at the eastern end of the Mediterranean Sea where Asia, Europe, and Africa come together

Centurion - an officer in the Roman army in charge of 100 soldiers.

Christ - The title of Jesus which means 'anointed' or 'chosen one' in Greek. The Hebrew word for Christ is 'Messiah". Jesus Christ is God's chosen one to bring salvation to his people.

Church - a group of the followers of Jesus that meets in a certain place. Jesus calls the church his body. Most of the books of the New Testament are letters to churches.

Circumcise - To remove the foreskin of the male sex organ. This was done to symbolize the removal of evil. It was also a sign of the covenant or agreement between God and the people of Israel.

City of Refuge - A place of safety for someone who had accidentally killed someone.

Commandment - A rule or teaching that people should obey. God gives his people commandments to help them live a good life.

Consecrated - To make or declare sacred; set apart or dedicate to the service of the Lord. To make an object of honor or hallo.

(To consecrate a building to be a church)

Covenant - An agreement or set of promises, usually between God and his people.

One of the most important covenant promises in the Bible is when God says, "I will be your God, and you will be my people." There is trouble if either side breaks the covenant promises that bind them together.

Creation - God created, or made, the world and the entire universe.

It is all his creation. The Bible says everything God made was very good. All creation is now hurt by the sin in the world. But one day, God will make creations perfect again.

Crucify - To nail or tie a person to a cross until that person died. A cross was made of rough beams of wood nailed together in a cross shape. Jesus died by this method, which was usually used for criminals.

Curse - To wish that bad things happen to someone or something. God curses or makes bad things happen, only as a punishment for not obeying him.

David - A great King of Israel. God promised the members of David's family would rule a kingdom that lasts forever. Jesus was born from the family of David. He is the 'Son of David' who will rule Gods Kingdom forever.

Day of the Lord - A phrase used in the Bible for the time in the future when God will destroy evil.

Demon - A powerful evil spirit that works for Satan. Demons can sometimes control people. But Jesus has power over demons. He can make them come out of people.

Disciple - A follower; someone who believes, and does what his or her leader teaches. Jesus had 12 disciples to be his special helpers. Today anyone who follows Jesus is his disciple.

Elders - Older men who were leaders of Gods people.

Eternal - Forever; with no end . God is eternal. Followers of Jesus are given the gift of eternal life.

Faith - Sure belief and trust. Faith is being sure of what you hope for and certain of things even if you cannot see them. To have faith in Jesus means to trust him and believe what the Bible says about him.

Famine - A time when there is not enough food for people. A famine can happen for many reasons. Maybe not enough rain falls, or insects destroy the crops. Sometimes people are fighting a war instead of growing things to eat.

Fasting - Going without food for a period of time. In the Bible, fasting was usually done by people during a special time of praying to God, or to show sadness.

Feast - A special time of celebration and eating. In the Bible, feasts celebrated the ways God helped his people.

Firstfruits - The first crops that Gods people would collect from their fields and give to God. This was a sign that everything the land produce belonged to God. In the New Testament, Firstfruits is the first part of a blessing that is received as a promise of more to come.

Forgive - To not punish a person for something wrong he or she has done; to pardon someone. The great message of the Bible is that God forgives us. Jesus took the punishment for the things we have done wrong.

Galilee - The Northern part of the land of Palestine. Jesus grew up in the town of Nazareth in Galilee. He did a lot of his ministry in Galilee.

Gentiles - means 'nations.' A Gentile is anyone who is not a Jew. Gods' plan of salvation begins with the chosen nation of Israel, and then moves to include all the nations of the earth.

Glory - Greatness and majesty that people can see or sense; usually of

God.

Gods' Characteristic Names:

Jehovah - Jireh - The Lord will provide,
Jehovah - Nissi - The Lord is my banner,
Jehovah - Shalom - The Lord is Peace,
Jehozabad - (Jehovah Endowed),
Jehovah - Shamah - The Lord is there.

Gospel - means "Good news." The gospel is the message about how Jesus defeated evil. He died and then became alive again to make us new and give us hope for the future. The job of Jesus' followers is to share the gospel with people all over the world.

Grace - Showing love and kindness to someone who does not deserve it. The heart of the Bible's message is God's grace. He loves people and saves them even while they are still fighting against him.

Hades - The place of the dead

Hallelujah - means 'Praise the Lord!' This word is made by putting together two Hebrew words: Hallelu (meaning "praise) and Yah (for the name of God, 'Yahweh,' or 'the Lord')

Heaven - The place where God is, and where other spiritual beings live. The followers of Jesus have their loyalty, or

citizenship, in heaven because Jesus is there. But
this does not mean that God has given up on the
earth. According to the Bible, the struggle against
evil is now taking place in both heaven and earth.
One day God will destroy this heaven and earth.
He will 'shake' out all evil. The he will make
a wonderful place where everyone does what is
right; a new heaven and new earth.

Heir - The person who receives or inherits what belongs to a relative.
The heir usually inherited these things when the
relative died.. In the Old Testament, Israel was the
heir of God. Israel received the Promised Land as
an inheritance from God. In the New Testament,
Gods' people are also called heirs of God. They
receive the gifts of righteousness; eternal life; and
the Kingdom of God.

High place - A place of worship built on top of a hill . High places
were altars, stone, or wood poles usually used for
worshiping false gods.

Holy - pure, set apart for God. God is Holy. He is perfect. He does
not do anything wrong. God also wants his people
to be holy one day God will make them perfect.

Holy Spirit - One of the three persons of God. In the Old Testament
we see the Holy Spirit active in the creation of the
world. The Spirit also filled certain people with

power at special times. It is the Holy Spirit that worked through men to produce the Scriptures. Because Jesus died and rose to new life, the Holy Spirit now lives in all Gods' people. He is the One who makes them new, teaches them, and gives them freedom for a new life.

Idol - Anything that is worshiped instead of the true God. In Bible times, idols were often statues of false gods made of wood, stone, or metal. Idolatry is the worship of idols.

Incense - A collection of spices that is burned to worship God. Incense produces a sweet smell. The Bible teaches that the prayers of Gods' people are like incense to him.

Iniquity - Guilt contracted by sinning. Actions which is not just.

Israel - A name meaning 'he struggles with God'. God gave this name to Jacob after he fought with and angel of God. The 12 tribes of the nation of Israel are from the family of Jacob (Israel). A member of the nation of Israel is called and Israelite. See also the word Jew in this dictionary.

Jacob - Son of Isaac, grandson of Abraham. Jacob was the father of the 12 tribes of Israel.

Jerusalem - The most important city in Israel. In Bible times, Jerusalem was the capital and also the place where the temple of God was built. Jerusalem is sometimes called 'Zion' 'City of David' or 'City of God.' Jesus cried about Jerusalem because the people did not know he was the Messiah. In the future, God will show us a New Jerusalem.

Jesus - A Greek name which means 'Savior'. Jesus is a from of the Hebrew name 'Joshua' which means 'The Lord saves'. When the Son of God was born as a human being, he was named Jesus. This is because he came to save his people from their sins. Jesus is one of the three persons of God. Jesus is also a real human person. Jesus will come to earth again to bring salvation to those who are waiting for him.

Joshua - A leader of the people of Israel. Joshua led the Israelites into the land God had promised them.

Judah - One of the sons of Jacob, and father of one of the tribes of Israel. The tribe of Judah was the main one in the southern part of the nation of Israel. When the nation split into two parts, the southern part was called Judah. Jesus was born from the tribe of

Judah.

Judge - A strong leader of the people of Israel before Israel had kings. God brought Judges to power to save the people from their enemies.

Justify - to make a person right with God. To justify is to say that someone's sins will not be held against him. The followers of Jesus are justified because Jesus died and rose again for them.

Kingdom of God, Kingdom of Heaven - Gods' rule, or reign, over everything He has made. The kingdom of God comes when God removes evil and brings real peace and justice. The main subject of Jesus' teaching was the kingdom of God. By becoming a follower of Jesus, a person becomes part of the Kingdom of God. When God's rule over the world is complete, the Kingdom will last forever.

Lamb of God - Jesus is call the Lamb of God. He was sacrificed like a lamb to take away the sins of Gods' people. See also the word Passover.

Law - this word is used in different ways in the Bible: 1) The first five books of the Old Testament are called the Law. They contain all Gods' rules for how Israel was to worship Him and live together as His people. 2) All the moral rules God gave His people in the Old Testament are called the law. Because of the sinful nature of all people, this holy law of God could not produce righteousness. So Jesus gives a right standing with God as a gift to his people. 3) Law can refer to all practical instruction God still want His people to obey. This law helps people show their love for God. It tells them how to live together peacefully. Real freedom is found in keeping God's perfect law. This is the new command to love one another.

The Law and the Prophets - a name for the entire Old Testament.

Leprosy - the word used in the Bible for different skin diseases and infections.

Levite - A member of the family line of Levi, one of the sons of Jacob. All priests came from the tribe of Levi. Other Levites worked in the temple and were teachers of the law.

Lord - is used in this book to refer to Jehovah God. But usually it is used for Jehovah God as a title showing His power over all things. The early followers of Jesus said 'Jesus is Lord' to mean that He has authority over everything. The Hebrew word for this name is Yahweh, which means. 'I Am Who I Am'. This name tells us that God is always with his people.

Lord's Supper - a meal shared together by the followers of Jesus. Bread is shared to remember the body of Jesus that He gave up to them. Wine is shared to remember His blood that was poured out for the forgiveness of their sins. The Lord's Supper helps the followers of Jesus remember three things; 1) Jesus died for them; 2)Jesus is alive and is with them now through His Spirit; and 3)Jesus will eat and drink with them again when He returns. Sometimes, the New Testament uses the words 'breaking bread' for the Lord's Supper. The Lord's Supper is also called Communion or the Eucharist by some followers of Jesus.

Manna - means 'What is it?' Manna was the name the Israelites gave the special food God provided to them in the desert. It was a white, bread-like, sweet tasting food that would show up on the ground in the morning. Jesus says He is like manna. He is the bread of life that can truly fulfill Gods' people.

Mediator - a person who helps bring peace between two or more people who are having conflict. Jesus is the mediator between God and people.

Messiah - A Hebrew word meaning 'anointed' or 'chosen one.' The Greek word used in the New Testament for 'anointed' is Christ. In the Old Testament. God promised to send a special person called the Messiah. This new king would save Gods' people. The New Testament show us that Jesus is the Messiah. He is God's chosen one to save His people.

Miracle - Any great show of power that goes beyond the usual laws of nature. God's miracles are wonderful signs of His power to make things right. Satan and his helpers sometimes do miracles to fool people.

Moses - A great leader of the people of Israel in the Old Testament. Moses led the people out of slavery in Egypt, and brought God's law to them. Later, he directed them through the desert. Moses died just before the Israelites entered the Promised Land. The New Testament writes about Moses as a faithful leader who pointed forward to the time of Christ.

Mystery - A secret, or something too hard to understand, that is revealed or explained by God.

Noah - A righteous man who believed God. He obeyed when God told him to build a huge boat (the ark) because a flood was coming.

Offering - something given to God to worship him. In the Old Testament, God's people offered food and animals to God. In the New Testament, Jesus offered himself as a sacrifice to God for us. The followers of Jesus serve God with their whole lives as an offering of praise to God.

Ordained - to officially make (someone) a minister, priest, rabbi, etc. To officially establish or order (something). God ordained the Levites to be the ministers of His people.

Parable - A short story that is told to show how one thing is like another. Most of the parable in the Bible are stories used by Jesus . These parables teach us what the Kingdom of God is like.

Passover - A Jewish celebration feast. It reminds the people how God saved them from slavery in Egypt. Part of the meal includes the Passover Lamb. At the first Passover, a lamb was killed and it's blood was placed on the people's door frames. This is so God would 'pass over' the homes of His people, and spare the lives of their first born sons. Jesus is the Passover Lamb for all of God's people. He was sacrificed so His people could be saved from sin and death.

Paul - a great apostle and leader among the first followers of Jesus. Paul was known first as Saul. His name was changed to Paul after Jesus appeared to him and he became a follower of Jesus. Paul had a special

job of bringing the good news of Jesus to the
Gentiles. Paul wrote many of the letters that make
up the New Testament.

Peter - One of Jesus' 12 disciples. He later became an apostle and
leader in the church at Jerusalem. Jesus changed
Peter's name from Simon to Cephas (which in
Greek is Peter). Peter once denied that he knew
Jesus. He later became a bold leader and was
thrown in jail for his faith.

Pharisees - means 'the separate ones.' In New Testament times, the
Pharisees were the main religious leaders of the
Jews. The Pharisees believed in following the Old
Testament laws very carefully. They also added
many of their own rules. Jesus often had trouble
with the Pharisees.

Priest - A person who brought sacrifices and prayers to God for all the
people. In Israel, a priest had to be from the tribe
of Levi. The high priest had special jobs to do.
He was the most important religious leader. The
New Testament tells us that Jesus is the high priest
for his followers. He gave himself as a sacrifice.
Now, all the followers of Jesus are priests. They
can freely bring their sacrifice of praise to God.

Prophet - A person God has chosen to bring His message to the
People. God often called the prophets 'my
servants', Sometimes God gave the prophets a

message about what would happen in the future. False prophets gave the people a message that really was not from God. True prophets always said that God was faithful to his promises. They told the people to be faithful. Jesus came to earth as a great prophet.

Psalm - means 'song'.   In the Bible, God's people used psalms to: Praise God, Cry out to God for help during trouble, and Thank God.

Ransom - The price paid to free someone who has been condemned. Jesus gave Himself as a ransom. He set His people free from slavery to sin, and its death penalty. See also (redeem)

Reap - To gather a crop at harvest time. Reap can also refer to what will happen to someone as a result of their own actions.

Reconcile, reconciliation - to bring peace between two people who have been enemies. The world sinned and was hostile towards God. Then God sent Jesus to reconcile the world to God.

Redeem, redemption - When a family member pays a price to buy a price to buy someone or something back from slavery or ownership by someone else. In the New Testament our brother, Jesus, redeems us

from sin, or sets us free, by His death on the cross.
See also (ransom)

Remnant - A few people that are left over from a bigger group. The
Bible says many people will fall away from
serving God. But God promises to always keep a
faithful remnant of those who are true to him.

Repent, repentance - To turn away from sin and start to follow God
completely. To repent means to change the
direction of one's life.

Resurrection - coming back to life after being dead. Death came into
the world because of sin. Jesus raised people from
the dead as a sign of God's power over sin.

The resurrection of Jesus is the key victory over death. Because
Jesus rose from the dead, His followers have
a new life now. They will also rise again with
new bodies when Jesus comes again. At the final
resurrection, all people will rise from the dead to
be judged by God.

Reveal, revelation - to show somebody something or teach them
something they did not know. In the Bible, god
reveals the truth about us and our world. By his
great act of salvation, God showed His people his
power and love. God sometimes revealed things
to certain people (prophets or apostles). When

Jesus came He revealed who God is and how much He loved us.

Righteous, righteousness - doing what is right or holy; being faithful to the promises of a covenant God is the only purely righteous one. God expects His people to also be righteous. But they do not always live by God's law. God sent Jesus so that those who believe in Jesus will have His righteousness given to them. The Holy Spirit now works in the followers of Jesus so they can live righteously.

Sabbath - a time of rest or ceasing to work. In the Old Testament, God told His people to celebrate Sabbath days (the 7th day of the week and other holidays). The land was to have a Sabbath year of rest every 7th year. Jesus often had conflict with the religious leaders of his day about the Sabbath. They had added many rules about what people should not do on the Sabbath. The Sabbath is a picture of the rest and peace Jesus' followers have because of his work for them.

Sacrifice - An offering or gift given to God to remove the guilt of sin. Throughout the Old Testament. God's people brought sacrifices to God. The greatest sacrifice was when Jesus gave His own life to pay for sin, once and for all. God's people today give themselves as a 'living sacrifices' to serve and praise God.

See also the word (Offering).

Sadducees - A small but powerful group of religious leaders at the time of Jesus. The Sadducees were mostly priests who followed only the Old Testament law. They did not obey the rules.

Salvation, save - to be rescued from danger or evil. Salvation is a main idea in the Bible. God will take away all the results of sin. He will bring His creation to a peaceful and friendly relationship with Him. The New Testament shows us that Jesus is the Savior. Only He can save us and our world.

Samaritan - A person from the country of Samaria (part of Palestine). The Samaritans were hated by the Jews because they had married non-Jew. They also worshiped God differently from the Jews. But Jesus showed His love for the Samaritans by going to them and teaching them about the Kingdom of God.

Sanctify - To make holy; to set apart to be used by God. The followers of Jesus are made holy by Jesus' sacrifice for them. But they must also keep on working to be sanctified. The Holy Spirit helps

Gods' people live Holy lives.

Satan - means 'enemy'. Satan is the enemy of God. He wants to destroy everything God has created. He is also called the devil, the evil one, the prince of this world and the god of the age. Satan brought evil into the world. He lies, destroys, and attacks the people of God. Jesus came into the world to renew what Satan had destroyed. Satan tried to stop Jesus, but Jesus is Gods' Son, and he has more power than Satan. The followers of Jesus can resist Satan by asking for the power of the Lord. God will one day win a complete victory over Satan. God is not a dictator; He has given us a mind to choose our leader.

Sin - Breaking Gods' law. Sin comes from a broken relationship with God. Sin is not a part of our original human nature. God created the first people with the ability to choose whether or not to trust and obey God. But now, all people are born with a sinful nature that holds them in slavery. This leads to all kinds of lawbreaking. God sent Jesus to defeat the power of sin and remove the punishment for sin. When God's people confess their sins God will forgive them. In the future, God will take away all the results of sin from his creation.

Son of Man - A title Jesus used for Himself during His ministry on earth. In the Old Testament, there is a prophecy about a divine person, 'one like a son of man.' This person would receive an everlasting kingdom, and be worshiped by all nations. Jesus called Himself 'the Son of Man. This showed that He had the authority and power of a divine person, and yet also was a man.

Synagogue - A Greek word meaning 'to gather.' The Jews gathered at buildings called synagogues to worship God and to study the Scriptures. Each Jewish community also used the synagogue to teach young people. Jesus went to the synagogue to worship. He also taught there. Paul used the synagogue as a place to preach the gospel to the Jews.

Tabernacle, Tent of Meeting - Tabernacle means 'dwelling place.' It was a special tent where the Israelites worshiped God. It is sometimes called the Tent of Meeting. It was a the place where God would meet His people. The Israelites used the tabernacle until Solomon built the temple. The tabernacle built on earth was a copy of the true tabernacle in heaven. Now because of Jesus sacrifice, His followers can enter the heavenly tabernacle. They can truly meet God When Jesus came to earth God was again dwelling with His people. Jesus brought peace between God and His people. So God will one day make His home with them again.

Teacher of the Law (also called a Scribe) - An expert in the law; a person with special training to read and write well. At first, scribes were people who wrote papers for others. By the time of Jesus, they were like lawyers. They were experts in using and teaching the Jewish law.

Temple - A building where people worship divine beings. God told Israel to build him a temple and worship Him there. God showed His people that He was with them by having His presence in the temple. In the New Testament, we learn that the new temple is not a building. God's people are now the temple of God. God's Spirit lives within them.

Tithe - means 'a tenth,' In the Old Testament, God's people would give a tenth of their crops of animals to God. This was a sign that God owned the land and had blessed His people. Also, the tithe would be used to support the priests and Levites, and to help the poor.

Unclean - A person or thing that did not meet certain conditions. Something unclean could not be part of religious services. God set the conditions for people and things to be included in worshiping Him. People who were unclean could be cleansed. Then they could worship again. To be unclean was a symbol for not being spiritually pure. The sacrifice of Jesus makes His followers spiritually clean. So they do not follow the Old Testament laws about unclean conditions.

Vision - A dreamlike experience that God uses to bring a message to someone.

Woe - Great suffering, pain, or sadness.

Worship - means 'to bow down.' Worship is an act of highest respect. Worship is

praising and serving someone who is worthy. The Bible teaches that only God is worthy of worship. The heart of human sin is worshipping and serving something instead of the true God. God's people joyfully praise and thank God when they are in His presence. The followers of Jesus give their whole lives as worship to God.

Wrath - strong anger. God's wrath is His great anger that comes when people will not stop sinning. This wrath leads to punishment of sin. God's people are saved from the wrath of God. They trust in His mercy, and are faithful followers of Jesus. For now, God is patiently holding back His wrath. Now is the day of salvation.. This is the time for people to repent. But one day, the great wrath of

God against sin will be fully unleashed.

Zion - A hill within the city of Jerusalem. God's temple was built on Zion. Sometimes Zion or Daughter of Zion is used to refer to the whole city of Jerusalem, or to the people of God. The New Testament refers to mount Zion as the New Jerusalem. It is part of the new heaven and new earth that we will see in the future.

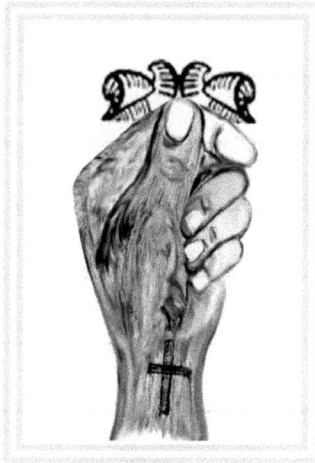

Create points to quote the
Word of God into your daily prayers:

Create points to quote the

Word of God into your daily prayers:

Remind God of His Promises:

Remind God of His Promises:

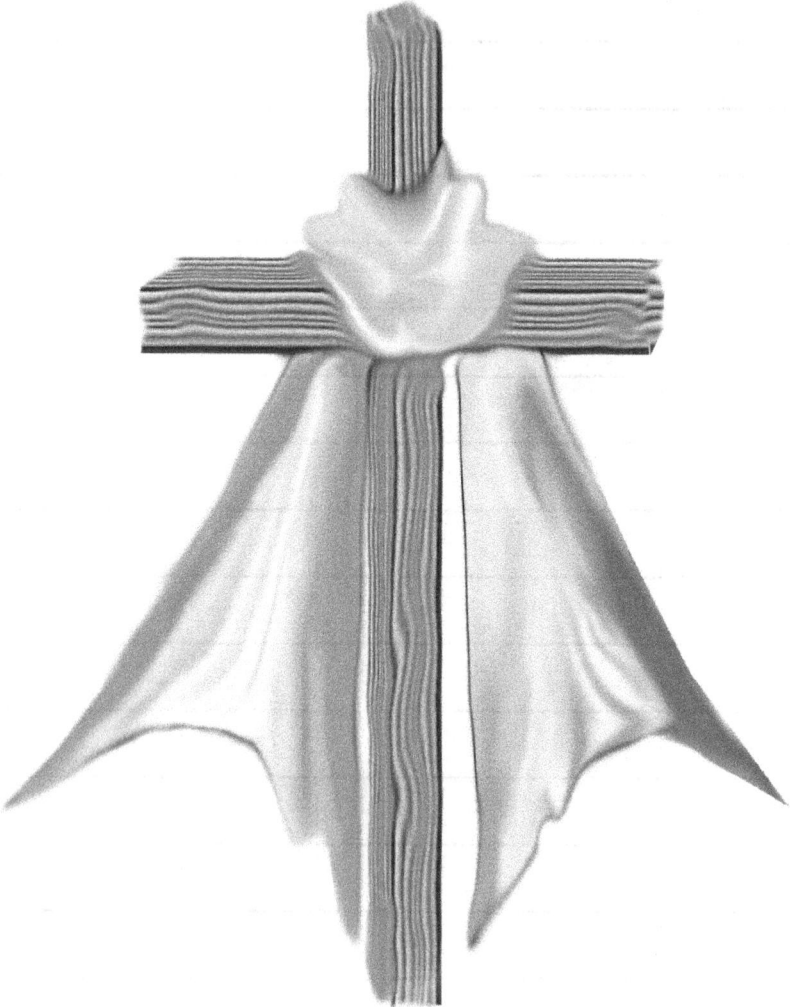